TOXIC
WORKPLACE
SIGNS

LEON LYONS

Mindset Mastership,

London, United Kingdom 2022

ABOUT THE AUTHOR

Leon Lyons is a British-born, Amazon best-selling author, a Psychological expert, and Senior Life Coach at Mindset Mastership, based in London, England.

Leo as he's known to friends used to consult global brands headquartered in central London. Although now he would say he found a more fulfilling role in life: coaching clients from around the world, changing lives for the better, and when he's not traveling or surviving global pandemics, he also writes about how success can happen.

Leon Lyons has now published 5 books:

1. How To Change Habits
2. Change Mindset, Behaviour & Positive Thinking
3. How To Find Work You Love
4. Rewire Your Brain: 2 Books in 1 Master Your Mindset & Habit Hack
5. Negotiation Skills: Techniques, Tactics

These five are his first books, with many others being published within weeks. Therefore, please also follow his Amazon author profile for future updates.

Here at Mindset Mastership, we help you understand what human behavior really is, and how to maximise your full potential. Whether you are stuck in business, lifestyle, dating or social life; we are here to coach and mentor you to achieve results. We have trained many clients across the globe to make radical changes to their thinking, behavior and mindset.

We are in the changing lives business.

Join Our

Personal Self-Growth

Power Group

To help reinforce the learning's from our books, I strongly suggest you join our well-informed powerhouse community on Facebook.

Here, you will connect and share with other like-minded people to support your journey and help you grow.

>>>**Click here to join Our Personal Growth Support Group** <<<

https://www.facebook.com/mindsetmastership

Dedicated to my ever-loving self-growth hackers at

https://www.facebook.com/mindsetmastership

FOLLOW US ON INSTAGRAM:

@MINDSETMASTERSHIP

TOXIC

WORKPLACE

SIGNS

LEON LYONS

WANT A COPY OF MY NEW BOOK?

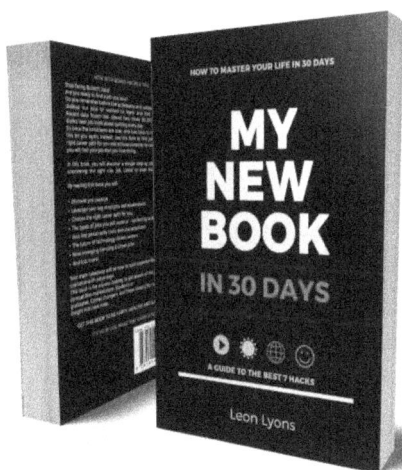

Email "TOXIC WORKPLACE SIGNS" TO:

MindsetMastership@gmail.com

MASTERSHIP BOOKS

UK | USA | Canada | Ireland | Australia
India | New Zealand | South Africa | China

Mastership Books is part of the United Arts Publishing House group of
companies based in London, England, UK.

First published by Mastership Books (London, UK), 2021

Cover design by Rich © United Arts Publishing (UK)
Text and internal design by Rich © United Arts Publishing (UK)
Image credits reserved.
Colour separation by Spitting Image Design Studio
Printed and bound in Great Britain

National Publications Association of Britain
London, England, United Kingdom.
Paper design UAP

A723.5

Title: Toxic Workplace Signs

Design, Bound & Printed:

London, England,
Great Britain.

"Until you make the unconscious

conscious, it will direct your life

and you will call it fate."

Carl Jung

Contents

CHAPTER 1: PREVENTION IS BETTER THAN A CURE

Identifying Red Flags in a Toxic Workplace and What to do About It

It is true, toxic workplaces have been on the rise for a long time. With an alarming number of employees suffering from burnout, we must all pause and take a long, hard look at our operating environment. However, if an employee begins to struggle with their job and is dissatisfied, how can they determine whether the problem is with them or the workplace? Have you ever felt as if the air in your office was suffocating? Is there conflict? Are deadlines looming, and do people appear stressed? We identify warning signals of a toxic workplace, investigate the variables that contribute to it, and offer advice on combatting such an atmosphere in this book.

What does "toxic work environment" mean?

In a toxic workplace, employees find it difficult to work or grow in their positions due to the unwelcoming climate favored by their coworkers, bosses, or the corporate culture. The term "toxic workplace" stretches back to the late 1960s. The definition was enlarged in the 1980s to encompass workplace behavior and laws. The term gained popularity after Virginia K. Baillie used it in her book, "Effective Nursing Leadership: a Practical Guide" to call attention to nurses' poor daily working conditions. She disclosed the norm, dictating how nurses were expected to behave – to possess leadership abilities and a compassionate attitude – and went on to demonstrate how

1

detrimental they were. These guidelines were so tight that they contributed to unhealthy work conditions, sexism, and discrimination. And as you will see in the following section, there is little difference between today's poisonous environment and Bailie's day.

What is a hazardous work environment?

The relationship of everyone (employees, management, and CEOs) to these factors affects whether a work atmosphere becomes healthy or toxic. They can have serious long-term repercussions, including career burnout.

Goals

Healthy work environment - Clear, obvious

Toxic work environment - Obscure, unclear

Values/beliefs/attitudes

Healthy work environment - Considered

Toxic work environment - Obscured, irrelevant

Roles

Healthy work environment - Clear, agreed upon

Toxic work environment - Ambiguous, unclear, conflicting

Communication

Healthy work environment - Supportive, assertive, understanding

Toxic work environment - Defensive, aggressive, passive-aggressive

Decision making

Healthy work environment - Based on agreement, including everyone's input

Toxic work environment - Top-down, one-way communication

Feelings

Healthy work environment - Expressed, discussed

Toxic work environment - Neglected or acted out

Listening

Healthy work environment - Active

Toxic work environment - Alternating monologues

Self-disclosure

Healthy work environment - Open, expressive

Toxic work environment - Closed, hiding

Conflicts

Healthy work environment - Resolved

Toxic work environment - Avoided

Human resources

Healthy work environment - Staff treated as a resource

Toxic work environment - Staff is valued

Task completion

Healthy work environment - Autonomous, left to the employee

Toxic work environment - Single right way, imposed by supervisors

Unclear goals and no transparency

A company's progress is determined by its goals. When everyone understands the company's objectives and their own smaller, personal ones, there is the potential for a healthy work environment to develop. Individuals understand their roles in the larger scheme of things, which keeps them busy and happy. Employers use a goal tracker to keep track of what each employee accomplishes, which aids in transparency.

A poisonous workplace lacks direction. Or it had long forgotten about them in the pursuit of growth and financial gain. On a lesser scale, individual staff objectives are ambiguous and poorly conveyed. This results in feeling disoriented in the work path as if they were standing still and underutilizing their talents.

EXAMPLE

Everyone appears to be constantly engaged in some aspect of a project within a workplace, but individual ambitions are seldom expressed openly. Thus, each individual is aware of the activities of their immediate coworkers, while the bigger project objectives remain veiled. It happens in the absence of straightforwardness that individuals feel they are moving like certifiable headless chickens.

Every workplace benefits from complete openness. It ensures that employees are on the same page about small and large goals and feel their participation is meaningful. This may be a breeze with time and project monitoring software, resulting in long-lasting beneficial benefits.

Values, beliefs, and attitudes are imprecise

Nowadays, this is generally referred to as "business culture." A good work environment is one in which values,

4

attitudes, and views are openly expressed and addressed. Everyone is made aware of the corporate culture at work, and prospective candidates are briefed in advance to guarantee a good fit. It's seldom evident what the company culture comprises in a hazardous work environment because values and beliefs are impenetrable and never spoken.

Roles are ambiguous
This factor may be the most significant in transforming a healthy workplace into a hazardous one. Whenever a worker knows their job, it shows that they comprehend what the work requests of them, i.e., what is generally anticipated and what makes for achievement or disappointment in undertakings. Once the lines become muddy, individuals can progressively lose sight of which duties (or behaviors) will advance their careers. They have lost sight of their responsibilities and what is expected of them.

This is frequently the case in smaller or growing businesses that lack the necessary labor to cover all elements of the organization. However, it is also evident in large firms, where management assigns and removes responsibilities arbitrarily to patch up bad leadership. Rather than hiring new staff, some firms choose to expand the functions of the existing personnel (most often without proper financial compensation).

EXAMPLE
1. When a CEO's assistant is unexpectedly tasked with making coffee for clients and acting as a personal errand boy.
2. In a tiny startup, the programmer is also expected to take on QA responsibilities because the company

cannot afford to engage more staff. This process continues for an entire year.

Only one-way communication is possible

A supportive environment fosters open, assertive communication. Appropriate communication is predicated on an awareness of the roles, objectives, attitudes, and beliefs outlined above. Understanding each person's function and hierarchy enables you to accomplish greater achievements.

Communication is never two-way in a poisonous environment. It is used to assert dominance or to engage in a power conflict. It's either passive-aggressive or passive or aggressive on its own.

- Passive-aggressive – expressing dissatisfaction without expressing it directly (eye-rolling, crossing arms, sarcasm, gossiping, and plotting)
- Passive – avoiding confrontation and communication entirely
- Aggressive – emotional outbursts, demanding authority over the conversing partner

EXAMPLE

1. (with a sarcastic tone) "Certainly, I have all the time in the world for additional meetings."
2. When confronted, the individual withdraws and silently agrees to all remarks, even those they disagree with.
3. An aggressive boss, for example, would reprimand an employee for making a mistake rather than focusing on resolving the issue.

Only top-down decisions are made

In a healthy workplace, decisions are made collaboratively, with participation from all parties. In comparison, there is no consensus on tackling a problem in a hazardous work environment. The decision is made by a superior without input or consultation from peers (who understand the situation better).

EXAMPLE

A programmer encounters a problem with the code, which may cause the project to run late. The team chooses to convene and determine the best course of action: whether they require an extension or can still reach the deadline. Their project manager can gain an objective perspective of the situation and discover a solution with the help of other programmers' opinions and ideas.

In a toxic environment, this same programmer would attempt to express the issue but be rejected. The project manager would then determine whether the programmer should work overtime or devise a "workaround" to fulfill the deadline.

Feelings are suppressed rather than expressed

Contrary to popular belief, expressing one's emotions in the workplace should be encouraged as long it is done self-assuredly and consciously. Given the variety of scenarios we encounter during our employment, it's reasonable that most of them will elicit a range of emotions. Additionally, staff should be encouraged to express and act on them openly.

Employees are expected to accept everything in a toxic work environment. There is a widespread dread of expressing themselves for fear of repercussions from coworkers or managers. This results in bottled-up frustrations, resulting in a lack of focus, a decline in productivity and happiness in the near term, and a deterioration of mental and physical health in the long run.

EXAMPLE

A significant deadline is looming, and everyone is working nonstop to meet it. One employee wants to express her worry and feelings about the impossibility of meeting the deadline and their collective exhaustion. Nevertheless, she cannot do so because of the stigma attached to such fears. She withdraws to the restroom multiple times a day to cry quietly and continually questions every decision she makes. This significantly complicates her work, and even simple activities take longer.

Listening is passive

When two people are conversing in a good work setting, one listens intently while the other speaks. Obviously, in a poisonous work atmosphere, the listener merely waits their turn to speak. There is no connection in either directions.

Self-disclosure is either absent or has devolved into excessive sharing

When we discuss self-disclosure in general, we are referring to the act of disclosing personal information to others. However, it is necessary to note that this statement has a slightly different meaning in the workplace. It's not about relating anecdotes from your family reunion or how your partner failed to do the dishes the night before, resulting in a fight. Self-disclosure in a professional context is about sharing your current wants and needs. Self-disclosure in a healthy workplace requires following our promises, such as "I will finish the task by 5p.m.," or communicating our immediate emotions, such as "I believe the office is a little stuffy, don't you think?"

Everyone remains mainly silent in a poisonous work atmosphere, minding their own business and rarely reacting to situations or expressing thoughts. This can breed a great deal of distrust among staff.

Conflicts are destructive and ineffective

Conflicts are never either positive or bad. There are essential differences in approaches, attitudes, or perspectives. Whether a disagreement is positive or negative is determined by how others respond. A healthy work atmosphere is unafraid of disagreement. It is viewed as offering possibilities to circumvent obstacles that would have otherwise weighed the project down. Individuals are urged to talk honestly and assertively, always keeping the end goal in mind. The ultimate goal is to arrive at a win-win situation.

A poisonous work atmosphere either overlooks or flees disagreement. Employees are not taught how to respond; and as a result, they devolve into fights that must be won. This contributes to the negativity of confrontations where one party's wants are met while the other party's are not. The victor (whether correct or incorrect) can be viewed as the more dominant individual. The losing party may desire retaliation, which will have a detrimental effect on them and the workplace.

Human resource primacy

Employee perceptions of the company's interest in their well-being, health, and contentment are considered of importance, whether the employee is regarded as valuable or a resource to be handled. Employees frequently feel that their bosses and managers are using them as tools to get the job done in a hostile workplace. They are shifted from department to department, their roles continuously changing depending upon the work at hand. Additionally, employees are taught to believe that sick days and vacations

9

are a burden to the company's success rather than a chance to rest.

Successful accomplishment of a task

A healthy atmosphere enables people to be self-sufficient in their employment. While guidelines should govern how things are done, people should be free to operate within them and make their own day-to-day decisions. The more autonomous they are, the more accurate the results.

There is only one way to accomplish things in a toxic work environment; it is usually one determined by the higher-ups. The system is constantly reinforced, and there is little to no opportunity for experimentation.

This exercise results in numbness, motivation loss, and a growing sense of being nothing more than "a cog in a machine." Employees are not expected to think critically or alter how things are done; rather, they are expected to listen, copy, and follow. When we examine workplace disagreements, one very intriguing thing becomes apparent. Liz Kislik, a management consultant with more than 25 years of experience, feels that confrontations are never the result of disagreements between two coworkers. She asserts that they are merely a symptom of deeper problems within the company.

What factors create a toxic workplace?

A workplace rarely deteriorates into a hazardous environment for employees on its own or out of the blue. Certain variables contribute to it. As they build and are ignored for an extended time, they result in a very unstable climate that begins to decay.

Undefined or unconsidered core values

It is not uncommon to see businesses proudly showcase their core values and goals. They have a vision for all website visitors to see without truly adhering to it. While they claim to foster a community of like-minded individuals dedicated to a common objective, the reality is quite different. There is a clear lack of direction, and it may appear as though everyone is doing their best without knowing why.

Inquire of yourself and your coworkers whether you are all aware of the big picture (aside from company growth). What ideals does the business wish to instill? Are they a success?

Company culture is nonexistent.

When it's nonexistent, it's as if you arrive to work every day, perform your eight to ten hours, and then leave. And it appears as though everyone else agrees. There is little informal conversation, and everyone appears to be focused on themselves and the work. You scarcely know the last names of your coworkers!

When a workplace culture is pursued to its logical conclusion, there are too many distractions: ping-pong or foosball tables, frequent company lunches, meetings every few hours, and chatting at desks. Employees are amused to boost their satisfaction at work - referred to as the "corporate kindergarten" informally, - when, in fact, the structure may be collapsing. What do people do during their workdays? Are they content to be here, or are they simply waiting for the clock to strike twelve so they can return home?

There is insufficient feedback

Returning to our healthy/unhealthy workplace discussion, how are employees expected to achieve when they are unaware of their duties and what determines success or failure on the job? Or are you going to learn? Businesses that fail to provide frequent feedback, performance reviews, or monthly meetings with their employees risk creating a circle of people. Is it customary to provide constructive criticism or conduct regular performance reviews? Consider how frequently you were informed of your errors and how to improve courteously and productively.

Established work habits are difficult to break (or not at all)

"But that's how it was always done when I first started!" "That is not how we were taught back in the day!" and "That isn't how we were instructed once upon a time!" are articulations regularly utilized by chiefs who won't improve. If you begin to hear this frequently, employee creativity and autonomy are likely questioned. And the more of this occurs, the faster people will begin to feel as if they are cogs in a machine. Unless a higher-up intervenes to question their choices, the workplace will likely become a breeding ground for toxicity. Are you and your employees being pushed to try new things? Is it permissible to pursue alternate methods of accomplishing tasks?

There is an excessive emphasis on output (and not nearly enough on people)

When a business is consumed by growth, the CEO may become determined to meet particular milestones quickly, neglecting everyone else. Everything must be improved, accelerated, or increased in size. Clients/customers come first, followed by the company and everyone else. This is followed by regular overtime stays, with the employer requiring that employees serve consumers and clients regardless of whether the call is the correct one.

This type of behavior results in stress, but it also generates tension and dread of failure, on top of the tiredness associated with extra work. Consider the last time you spent a vacation guilt-free. One where you may relax and unwind without worrying about the job that awaits when you return. Are individuals guilted or frightened to work longer hours to accomplish particular milestones?

Employees that are not a good fit
Even employees play a significant role in creating toxic work environments. So, what makes an employee so unfit that their behavior contributes to creating an unsafe work environment?
1. An unwarranted attitude of entitlement
2. Core beliefs opposed to those of the firm
3. The formation of cliques and groupings that are exclusive of others (as in high school)
4. Selfishness (they consider how each scenario can profit them alone, rather than the collective)
5. Gossiping and disseminating rumors or false information within the workplace
6. Passive-aggressiveness
7. Self-disclosure regarding personal matters (bring personal difficulties to work)
8. Assuming credit for others' work but never demonstrating initiative.
These are only a couple of poisonous working environment propensities. Some are indicative of emotional immaturities, such as clique formation and gossiping. However, some habits in toxic are oblivious to most, such as excessive sharing. It is critical to recognize and correctly

address them. Unfortunately, spotting toxic persons is frequently a matter of trial and error, particularly if you have never interacted with such individuals. You're likely to get burned a few times before mastering the art of seeing them from a distance.

How does a poisonous workplace appear?

A hazardous workplace can appear identical to a healthy one, at least on the surface. Additionally, one person may perceive a workplace as hazardous while another does not. This occurs due to an imbalance in how employees are treated or as a result of differences in work experiences. Individuals who have worked with toxic coworkers, managers, or entire work environments are more likely to recognize the warning signs sooner. However, for those who haven't, here are a few clear signs:

Thirteen questions to assist you in identifying a toxic workplace

Human resources specialist, Liz Ryan, who runs the Human Workplace blog, has outlined several telltale signals of an unhealthy workplace culture. Following her lead, we've developed questions to assist you in determining whether or not you're working in such an environment.

1. **Observe how people behave in and around the office.** Do they communicate, smile, and converse casually upon occasion? The absence of smiling and relaxed faces is a warning indicator.

2. **How tenaciously are you pursuing success?** When power takes precedence over individuals, frequent overtime, and weariness, bosses who focus on failures rather than triumphs are common.

14

3. **Is creative liberty and resourcefulness emphasized?** Employees are fearful of experimenting or working independently in a hazardous work environment. The higher-ups must run everything, and deviating from the established procedure is frowned upon.

4. **How are employees and supervisors/bosses communicating?** Do your managers and supervisors communicate well with one another? How about employees and supervisors? Inadequate or nonexistent face-to-face communication, missing CEOs, and power disputes in senior management are all issues that flow down to interns, polluting the entire workplace.

5. **What are people's attitudes toward their work?** If possible, inquire about your coworkers' feelings about their jobs. Are they content to be there, are their work assignments challenging, and do they believe they have room to grow? You may be asked the same questions. An emphatic "no" to more than one of these indicates the presence of a more serious issue.

6. **How are achievements and failures handled?** You'd be astonished at how much success has become normalized. It has gotten to the point that we no longer acknowledge it, preferring to focus on mistakes in the erroneous belief that only they can "make us better." This is detrimental to a company's culture, as achievement and acclaim propel us ahead. Note that criticizing others' failures is more prevalent than praising even the little victories.

7. **Is your perspective and that of your coworkers validated?** Consider how well you (and everyone else in your office) understand your jobs. Are you questioning your views when confronted with a problem? Are your

contributions and those of your coworkers valued and incorporated? Because a healthy workplace accomplishes this daily.

8. Is additional unneeded work being piled on? Consider whether you are being assigned tedious activities that are not part of the job description. You should accept when your manager asks you to help with quality assurance despite your sales role since you want to help your colleagues. Accepting out of fear of being fired, punished, or called out for not being a "team player" strongly indicates an unhealthy work environment. If you already have a lot on your plate, you should be able to decline assignments that aren't part of your job parameters.

9. Do any employees receive preferential treatment? Nowadays, favoritism comes in various shapes and sizes. The most well-known example occurs in businesses where certain employees are first and foremost buddies of the CEO or another member of higher management. There should be no instances where employees attend work lunches with their superiors because they are on better terms with them than others. This results in sharing information that is otherwise unknown to other employees, fostering the building of cliques and gossiping.

10. Is the office atmosphere tense and quickly agitated? Irritability is one of the most obvious indications. It is one of the first signs of burnout, and the closer someone is to "exploding," the more irritated they become over even the tiniest things. Observe how others behave during crunch times or even when debating duties and objectives. When a workplace places excessive pressure on its employees, they will snap at the mere mention of deadlines, changes, and modifications.

11. Is there sufficient and consistent feedback? A lack of feedback indicates a general lack of interest in employee career advancement. This is most likely a corporation unconcerned with growth as long as you assist them in achieving favorable results.

12. Is there a sense of community and belonging? While we mentioned that ping-pong tables, team building events, and in-office conga lines are all "kindergarten treatment," there is still a need for a sense of connection. After all, you are all working together for a minimum of eight hours per day. A poisonous workplace is one in which everyone works and entertains themselves on their computers or phones, sharing nothing and departing when their shifts are complete.

13. How frequently do "boomerang" personnel appear? It is unusual for a business to see rapid growth in a short period. When two to three people leave for a single post within a year or two, the atmosphere is almost certainly poisonous. New trainees struggle to adjust to the culture, but what if management sets unrealistically high requirements.

Watch out for red-flag language
Given that we've already discussed hazardous indications in the context of employment circumstances, we want to focus now on red flags. This is especially useful if there is no visibly hazardous environment but only unhealthy behaviors.

When doing a job interview, keep an eye out for the following:

- If you've noticed their job advertisements popping up frequently, inquire about it: "I've noticed you're frequently hiring." "Are you growing?" "How long have you been employed here?" This could be a clue that many individuals are stopping or regularly moving on.

- The hiring process moves too quickly (to fill a vacancy) or takes too long (you are not one of their first picks, so they leave you in the dark).

- Recruiters/employers appear to be distant and uncaring. They inquire about your background, objectives, and plans, focusing on what you have accomplished and what you can do for them.

- Recruiters/employers do not appear to be trying to pitch you on the position. They appear to be fine either way. This indicates an uninterested workplace that couldn't care less where your career takes you.

- Employers/recruiters constantly remind you how many candidates have applied for the same position. It's a ruse designed to make you nervous and susceptible to accepting a lowball offer.

- Recruiters/employers ask you questions that demonstrate a lack of understanding of your job. This commonly occurs when programmers and developers are questioned about several languages. In this type of job, you are likely to have shifted roles, be unclear about your objectives, and receive inadequate feedback.

- "We try sincerely and live it up!" Sugarcoating is almost certainly a widespread practice of forcing people to work overtime. Indeed, there are rules regulating labor hours. California's restrictions are among the most prominent, so checking if your area has similar ones will only help you.

- Recruiters/employers avoid responding to inquiries about work hours, promotions, or career advancement opportunities. There is no making way for progress, and they are very likely to contribute advancements and rewards "as they go" - without structure. Expect to work in an environment where you will almost certainly have to pursue the employer for them.

At your current workplace

Toxic situations arise as a result of toxic language. It is frequently the first and most obvious indication that you are in a negative environment. We've compiled a list of the most commonly encountered examples:

- "Are you the manager here, or am I?"

Alternatively, "I've been here longer than you have to know that... "

These statements are frequently used to assert control and coerce you into performing work in another manner.

- "Can you reschedule your vacation?" This is a critical period for the company."

Your rest time is non-negotiable. Vacations and sick leave are critical in maintaining a healthy mental state. While you should take care not to leave the workplace with an incomplete pile of work, no supervisor has the authority to order you to put your personal life on hold for the company's sake.

- "If you don't want this job, someone will gladly take it in your stead."

Due to its directness, supervisors are less likely to hear it. A coworker most frequently makes this comment, disguised as a well-intended "reality check." The purpose is to persuade you to refrain from expressing any negative ideas or reservations about how the workplace is run.

- "Stop creating excuses and simply perform what was requested."

If you have valid reservations about a work you've been assigned, they are not excuses. This reply stems from the belief that employees should always listen to their managers and never challenge their authority. If you are told this, understand that it is a tactic to assert power.

- Work is not supposed to be enjoyable — that is why it is referred to as 'work.'"

Work should be stimulating and demanding. It should be pleasurable. When you hear this, the person is attempting to eliminate any drive to alter your job routine. Or if you suggest a new method of doing things.

- I'm not fond of your attitude."

There is a distinction between having an attitude and asserting one's self-worth. Recognize when your superiors attempt to silence you due to their inability to handle legitimate criticism.

- "They/we can replace you at any time, so I'd be cautious if I were you."

This is a common form of intimidation employed to keep people in line. They understand that people require jobs and will resort to threats such as these.

- Look at _____; she's also dealing with personal issues/work-related troubles, yet she's not moaning!"

Simply because one of your coworkers does not practice self-disclosure does not mean that no one else should.
20

These remarks suppress uniqueness and effectively eliminate any attempt to call attention to improper workplace procedures.

Pro tip from Clockify: When in doubt about what constitutes oversharing and what constitutes self-disclosure, discuss it first with yourself and then make a choice. "I am not to blame; I was meant to do X/Y but failed to do so!" Constant finger-pointing exposes a more fundamental issue – employees are fearful of repercussions and accept responsibility. Rather than concentrating on finding a remedy, enormous lengths are made in identifying the cause or dissecting the error.

- "If no one complains about your work, you're doing well. Simply continue working."

While this statement might not appear hazardous, it contains numerous concealed ticking time bombs. Employees will unconsciously anticipate the arrival of a negative comment. Additionally, a lack of constructive feedback will quickly drive them into a rut. This type of statement enables supervisors to avoid the additional responsibilities of monitoring their employees' progress and providing timely feedback.

With these uncomfortable circumstances and dialogues, one has to ask how such environments affect us. After all, we are not robots but rational, emotional individuals.

Toxic employment environments are detrimental to mental health

The internet is replete with articles, videos, blogs, and now books confirming the detrimental effect toxic work settings have on mental health. You begin to lose sight of the breadth of your abilities and capabilities, minimize everything you do, and doubt whether you've ever been a good employee.

Apart from feeling defeated and doubting your abilities, prolonged exposure to toxic workplaces can be a more serious problem.

Depression
Is it possible for a poisonous work environment to cause depression? Yes, without a doubt.

Without detail, significant medical research has established how the depression caused by internal and external workplace issues impairs judgment, productivity, and career prospects.

How can you know whether a hazardous workplace is harming you?
We undervalue our bodies. They are adept at indicating when something is amiss, but we frequently miss them. We push ourselves, oblivious to warning signs and take our mental and physical health for granted until it is too late. This is particularly true in office settings, where we are continually exposed to low-level stressors that we disregard as normal.

Simply because we are accustomed to them does not make them normal or acceptable. As a result, to prevent falling into this trap, we've created a "health checklist." Utilize it to monitor your body daily and identify anything unusual early.

Note: This checklist is not intended to be a medically-approved method of self-diagnosing anxiety, depression, or other diseases. It is only a suggestion for self-inquiry and can be beneficial when consulting your physician. Consult a qualified physician if you are experiencing any major symptoms.

Checklist for mental and physical health:
- What kind of sleep are you getting? Do your resting hours differ from your typical schedule? How long has this been occurring?
- Do you experience bodily discomfort or suffering at the prospect of going to work or throughout your commute?
- How is your appetite? Is it out of the ordinary?
- Do you occasionally experience a sensation of foreboding, as though something horrible is about to happen? Is this something that occurs at work or home?
- Do you frequently feel depleted and exhausted? (despite adequate sleep)
- Are you having severe abdominal discomfort or headaches?
- Do you have trouble remembering even the tiniest details such as names, dates, and so on?
- Do you believe you've become more intolerant or irritable? Are you more apt to snap at friends and family?

If you've responded yes to several of these questions, you've likely experienced the negative effects of a toxic work environment. The best game plan is to talk with your doctor and decide the next steps. No measure of accentuation can be put on the fact that it is so basic to answer rapidly to try not to do harm.

Is it conceivable to sue your manager for establishing an unsafe workplace? Can the employer be sued for creating a hazardous work environment? While an unhealthy workplace might be detrimental to an individual's health, can a court case be built around it? The gaming business is notorious for its harmful workplace impacts. Game developers will burn out to the point where they may get illnesses, become sad, and require medicine, with some rendered unable to work for months. However, have their businesses faced legal action? Unfortunately, no. And here is why.

A business might be regarded as having violated the law if the following occurred:
1. Discrimination based on race, handicap, gender, age, religion, or sexual orientation
2. Sexual harassment (verbal or physical), and
3. Failure to respond to all claims and concerns of discrimination or harassment.

It's critical to remember that there is no legal basis for favoritism, workplace bullying, or financial hardship. To make a business or employer liable for legal action, they must commit a serious breach.

When is a toxic work workplace illegal?

While legislation varies by country, it can be claimed that mental and emotional suffering circumstances must be severe enough that a rational person cannot cope.

There are a few requirements for a complaint to be admissible in court, namely:
1. That the employer's conduct was out of control and scandalous
2. It was distressing because of the behavior
3. The pain was unbearable

Regrettably, only a few complaints meet these criteria. For instance, a supervisor or manager posting an unpleasant office Christmas photo of an employee on the water cooler is not deemed provocative or harsh enough. Yes, it produces embarrassment and distress, but not to the point where a person cannot cope mentally. So, if there are few to no legal avenues for correcting a toxic work environment, what are your options?

How to deal with a toxic workplace
Our responses to a malicious work environment are similar. According to Kislik, our amygdala (the primitive region of the brain) interprets emotional pressures as physical danger. Then it's unsurprising that our bodies respond with perspiration, tremors, palpitations, and an unexplainable yearning to flee. We experience the symptoms long before the unpleasant event or trade has a chance to be processed. The key to this is to practice maintaining a safe distance and approaching toxins logically.

Attempt to resolve the situation through dialogue
Suppose the issue is with a coworker. Why not attempt to resolve it verbally. Be aggressive and communicate from a position of understanding. Bear in mind that confrontations are not inherently negative, but our responses to them are. Make your best effort to fix the problem, then hand the rest over to the other side. And if all else fails, there's always human resources, whose duty is to help keep the workplace healthy.

After determining that your workplace is harmful, HR should be the first people you contact. In particular, if you're not sure who to trust at work, this is a good rule of thumb to follow.

Friends and family are generally the first to notice when something goes wrong in our professional lives. While we agonize over workloads, deadlines, and project milestones, they see the toll that stress takes on us. Lean on them and discuss your troubles; then seek an unbiased viewpoint. Those closest to you will discern if you are only moaning or whether there is a genuine issue at hand.

If you have work buddies and all have each other's best interests at heart, you're already one step closer to resolving the problem. You can discuss the work environment, relieve stress, and chronicle incidents and events together (if you need proof). And if you don't know anyone, attempt to create some acquaintances or look for those who appear to be going through similar difficulties.

However, if your group only discusses work-related difficulties and focuses on how horrible things are, it can soon evolve into something harmful. You are always rekindling the flames rather than addressing the matter. As the saying goes, "it is preferable to be safe than sorry." Document it when you have a distinct impression that someone's tone is nasty, toxic, or intended to chastise you. Conversations, email exchanges, and documents all serve to summarize the occurrence. Perhaps it appears severe, and you fear appearing paranoid; but it proves to be a valuable ace under your sleeve if things go wrong.

How to document:
- Immediately following an unpleasant event or conversation
- Recognize and document observed behaviors

- Keep track of dates and times. Keep track of time spent at work. Determine early on whether you are wasting time or your production has decreased.
- Screenshot emails and chat exchanges and store them somewhere private and secure

No one can tell when you will need verification, especially with justifiably conditions. Documentation is spurred by self-protection, not distrustfulness. It is generally smart to contact HR when you feel powerless. Speaking with a third party can be helpful when you're not sure whether confronting a problem or dealing with a certain individual would make things worse.

If there is no human resources department, communicate any concerns to your employer or a higher-up. If you are concerned about retaliation, request prudence and confidentiality.

Balance out the negative with the positive

Concentrate on self-care. If all you do at work is stress out, then return home and meditate on the day's events since it will only compound. Increase time spent on hobbies and interests or with family. Here are some suggestions:

- Plan or sign up for events throughout the week that you can look forward to
- Avoid working overtime beyond what is necessary
- Avoid multitasking
- When you return home, listen to your favorite music or watch soothing videos
- Take long showers or baths
- Journal your thoughts, allowing frustrations to flow out on paper (this helps verbalize your thoughts and clears your mind of them)

- Plan or sign up for events throughout the week that you can look forward to

There are numerous additional tips as self-care is unique to each individual. Determine which small self-indulgent activities work best for you and commit to them regularly. **Note:** Avoid hazardous habits such as excessive alcohol intake, self-medication, or binge eating. They will eventually exacerbate the symptoms.

Resign from the company

When all other options have been exhausted, depart. It is pointless to remain in an environment that is not only bad but also threatening for an entire eight hours. Your emotional and physical well-being are priceless. It is preferable to leave than risk permanent health problems. Simply be cautious of causing employer or coworker resentment by looking for a new job on the sidelines.

Toxicology in the workplace is more prevalent than it has ever been. Whether excessive or subtle, it causes physical and mental distress to employees and in the end, it costs companies money in the form of decreased productivity and sick leave. To overcome this, we need a level mind, a supportive environment (with family, friends, and coworkers), and a supportive job. While no single individual can make a company a better place, we can all learn how to guard our backs and keep our health intact.

Is Your Workplace a Dysfunctional Environment?
The Five Types of Toxic Cultures

Toxic work environments are riddled with hate, cliques, gossip, mistrust, and self-centered behavior. They foster dysfunction through ineffective communication, power battles, hostility, and abusive leadership. Collaboration, productivity, and invention suffer as a result, while fear, manipulation, and blame flourish. All of this undermines employee loyalty and leaves employees emotionally exhausted.

This comes as no surprise. Around the world, the Great Resignation and cancel culture is gaining popularity. Unhappy employees are quitting in droves now more than ever. The risk of remaining in hazardous employment outweighs the risk of being unemployed. According to SHRM, 58% of employees leave their jobs due to a toxic work environment, and the yearly cost of culture-related turnover is $223 billion. While there are other forms of toxic workplace cultures, the following are five that are extremely prevalent.

Hustle culture
Hustle is one of the most accepted work cultures, but it is frequently fraught with micromanagement. This profit-driven mentality is well-known for exploiting employees by requiring them to work longer hours for little pay. Being an enthusiastic specialist has been raised to a shallow focal point, with agents tolerating the assumption that the more hours they put in, the more valuable they are. Therefore, they put their emotional well-being and individual lives at

29

risk, forego breaks, and oppose taking PTO. Accordingly, the staff is extended excessively, ultimately wearing out.

Hayley Albright, senior brand and client experience supervisor at Xena Workwear makes sense when she claimed that "laborers often feel a sense of urgency to work extended periods because of tight cutoff times and stir stacking up. Because of the work lack and inordinate internet-based gatherings. They'll begin by responding to emails after hours and progress to working outside of typical business hours and over holidays. Eventually, this schedule takes its toll on the mind. Businesses must establish work boundaries and assist people in feeling no guilt about unplugging."

The culture of blame and "every worker for themselves"
A blaming culture does not extend to the top. When leaders refuse to accept responsibility for their actions, they set a precedent that mistakes are bad and unwelcome. As a result, nobody accepts responsibility out of fear of being chastised, losing their job, or appearing unprofessional. "That is not my responsibility" is a prevalent attitude in a blame culture. This has a detrimental effect on the workplace environment, but it also prevents people from committing to deadlines or expectations, allowing them to shift blame or accountability easily.

According to Matt Erhard, managing partner at Summit Search Group, "success is considered a scarce resource, and mistakes are perceived as personal failings rather than educational opportunities." Therefore, staff conceal botches or redirect fault instead of zeroing in on their endeavors when settling and issue and forestalling until later on. This promotes a "every man for himself" mentality in which employees are viewed as opponents rather than collaborators, leading to gossip, backstabbing, undermining, and other undesirable behaviors. "Trust relationships are then destroyed, and employees grow so anxious for positive attention that they turn to dishonest practices, such as taking credit for another's effort."

Clique culture

A clique culture is the polar opposite of an inclusive culture, as it fosters an environment in which people feel uneasy being themselves. This is because management and human resources fail to safeguard employees from improper jokes and comments on color, religion, gender, weight, age, place of origin, how one identifies, and social injustice issues, among other things.

Anyone who does not share the clique's attitude is excluded, made to feel invisible, and frequently targeted with bullying. As a result, employees feel alone. Cliques destabilize the team by obstructing communication, cohesiveness, and collaboration. Frequently, high achievers or members of cliques are held to lower standards than others.

According to Suzanne Wylde, a coach and author, "exclusion from an unseen inner circle is a prevalent kind of group toxicity." Perhaps one team member purposely excluded from specific emails or meetings is never solicited for their opinion, or is never invited to social events. It could be overt or covert, but it could also be a type of scapegoating — sacrificing one person's well-being to soothe the egos of others. This isolation can be extremely detrimental to a person's psychological well-being and is a kind of bullying."

Another well-known type of clique is the "bro culture," in which white male employees are perceived as superior to female employees. As a result, non-white men and women are excluded from decision-making. This "bro culture" permeates not just the technology industry but also sectors such as politics, banking, and finance. This results in women fighting for their worth and acceptance, enduring demeaning, sexist, and misogynistic comments, discriminatory and improper behavior, wage differences, and social exclusion. This all contributes to a toxic work climate for women.

An authoritative culture is built on the foundations of power and control. As a result, bullying and discrimination are widespread. A dominant culture is characterized by favoritism, nepotism, and "yes (wo)men." According to Jean Holthaus, LISW, LMSW, "in this culture, employees are punished for being honest either explicitly or implicitly. The person who speaks the truth is called a troublemaker, or the employee who dares to challenge the wisdom of their boss's new idea is passed over for promotion due to their lack of teamwork."

To keep control, leadership demonstrates its hierarchical authority. According to Hilda Wong, founder of Content Dog, "in authoritarian cultures, executives disregard employees' opinions and ideas, causing people to feel undervalued and disheartened in the firm." They keep employees in the dark because they believe people in non-management positions are beneath them and have nothing valuable to contribute. Employees learn about impending changes only after they have already occurred or via the rumor mill.

Fear-based society

32

Employees are encouraged to respectfully challenge methods, practices, and anything that isn't working in good company culture. Employees are intimidated, abused, gaslighted, and dominated in a fear-based culture. According to Logan Mallory, Vice President of Motivosity, "a fear-based culture is one of the most toxic workplace cultures because it fosters a hostile work atmosphere. Employees will do all possible to avoid repercussions, including avoiding risks and cutting costs."

Employees anxiety is heightened in a fear-based workplace where fear trumps trust, as they are constantly concerned about possible penalties or losing their jobs. This results in the following:

- Employees hesitant to speak the truth or report bullying, harassment, or misbehavior
- Employees too focused on daily goals rather than the larger picture
- Going to any length to appease their employer and avoid blame
- A rife rumor mill that seems more credible than what management and leadership communicate

Toxic Coworkers to Avoid (and How to Protect Yourself)

Learn how to deal with difficult coworkers

A single employee behaving badly at work can send company morale spiraling downward. Unfortunately, most businesses have multiple ne'er-do-wells who bring the entire organization down. It's time to call out that morale- and productivity-killing personalities so you can identify them and avoid their messes.

Every workplace has one (or two, or three!). You are aware of these sorts. Those poisonous employees are just concerned with themselves, regardless of the cost to their coworkers or the firms in which they work. The sort won't hold back to beat you to the punch by kowtowing to gain management's great graces. It can happen when you are next in line for an advancement, raise, or even a gesture of congratulations from the chief. Essentially, the individuals will step all over you and your coworkers to obtain their desired outcome (with as little work as possible).

Is it possible to advance while your office's ne'er-do-wells plot your demise? Yes. To be successful in today's business environment, you must detect your negative coworkers as soon as possible. Greed, sloth, self-centeredness, and backstabbing habits are all too prevalent in many corporate cultures. The people who represent this behavior inside associations regularly track partners, investing a legitimate day's energy while not lifting the heap. The time has come to get down on them.

If your mind is inundated with toxic colleagues you've experienced in the past (or are now dealing with), you are most certainly not alone. Furthermore, the days of simply grinning and bearing them are passed. Here are nine of the most prevalent types of bad colleagues to avoid and how to work around them by starting your own business.

The politician
Promotions based on merit are not a priority for schmoozers. Rather, they engage in office politics, popping into the boss's office every five minutes to proclaim their indispensability. The Politician gets absorbed by corporate politics. Their professional lives become a game where they are continually vying for the next job, promotion, or

project. On the other hand, they spend little to no effort on present projects.

To safeguard yourself: If you want to achieve the promotion you deserve without getting involved in office politics, start by evaluating your supervisor. If your boss has a large ego, Politicians will be difficult to defeat since they excel at stroking egos and kissing up to get what they want. If your supervisor is not an egomaniac, he or she will quickly tire of the exquisite displays. Once you've identified the motivating element, you can adjust your conduct to battle the Politician without losing sight of the task. The most effective approach is to state the facts. For the Politician, documentation and responsibility are akin to Superman's kryptonite. The proper documentation halts politicians in their tracks since they cannot spread their lies in the face of evidence that demonstrates who is performing the labor. Establish a paper trail. If possible, save all of your emails and voicemails. You may require them in the future.

However, when it comes to paperwork, keep in mind that politicians frequently utilize email. They request documents for evaluation and then forward them to the boss without your awareness. They enjoy creating the illusion that they have performed the task. A favorite strategy is to respond to you — naturally with a cc to the manager — but take credit for your work. Ascertain that the information flowing to the boss originates with you. Never give the Politician an opportunity to claim credit for work you created.

Coincidentally, it never harms to boast a tad around oneself. Make your presence felt and lay out your authoritative worth. Sound politicking might be advantageous to you.

The rooster

These are fascinating individuals. They are referred to be Roosters for two reasons. They appear to want to brag a lot about themselves, and they also enjoy hedging their bets to avoid having to choose. The Rooster is somewhat egocentric, which impairs their capacity to make decisions. If a Rooster makes a bad one, it's a serious affront to their ego. They may eventually have to admit their error. The Rooster's fear of imperfection keeps him on the fence. They seldom, if ever, make a choice. If they are fortunate, another will decide for them, or if they wait long enough, the decision will make itself. In any case, the Rooster's passive strategy enables them to maintain a degree of plausible deniability.

The Rooster is often quick to lay blame. They appear more interested in determining who is responsible for the problem than resolving it or determining its cause (not that they could resolve anything without choosing). The Rooster prefers to ignore issues, hoping they will resolve themselves.

How to safeguard yourself: There are two options available if you are forced to work with a Rooster. Either compel them to make a choice or tear down the fence and watch them run amok. Whichever path you take, you'll require a great deal of patience.

The funeral director

These individuals operate on negative energy and are motivated by adversity. Their days are consumed by drama. Although they typically have sufficient time to finish their allotted responsibilities, they procrastinate or otherwise delay progress until a crisis occurs and something "must be done." No matter the assignment, it will soon become the "end of the world" unless it is completed. How to safeguard yourself: When working with a Funeral Director, keep a flexible schedule. Assign a deadline that is early than the actual deadline. This will prevent their dilemma from becoming yours.

The tattletale

Do you ever wonder who maintains the office gossip mill? Or how your employer learns about every tiny mistake you and your colleagues make immediately after they occur? Consider your office tattletale as the culprit. While some people attempt to harbingers of good news, the Tattletale does not. They deal mostly in negative office gossip and rumors and any other information they believe may help them advance. They relish the opportunity to spread bad news if it concerns someone else and not them.

To safeguard yourself: Keep your lips shut and avoid disclosing anything you don't want the entire world to know. There is just one thing you can be certain of when dealing with Tattletales: they will discover any information you offer, presuming it will give them a competitive edge within the firm. Bear in mind that whatever you say to them has the potential to be used against you!

However, tattletales do have utility. If you wish to distribute information, simply inform your workplace tattletale and request that he maintain confidentiality. He will succumb to temptation, and your message will swiftly spread throughout the organization.

The points shaver

Each of us is familiar with a Points Shaver. They maintain a running tally of everything. Anything they do for you is logged on their mental scorecard, and they anticipate being reimbursed at some point — very soon!

Points Shavers appear to recall what they did but forget what you did for them. Whenever you request a favor, they launch into a litany of what they have previously done, and how your new demands would raise the debt you owe them. They've lost count of the number of times they've cashed in their favors.

How to safeguard yourself: Keep in mind that the score is never in your favor when working with a Points Shaver. Keep score only if it is worthwhile. The sanest course of action may be to avoid the Points Shaver entirely.

The office flirt

I accept that we are generally mindful of who this person is. In any case, watch for Office Flirts who teased in a 21st-century way. You may become embroiled in an email back-and-forth or instant messaging exchange that devolves into flirty behavior without your knowledge. Alternatively, you may receive dubious correspondence due to being the Office Flirt's Facebook or other social networking site buddy. The bottom line is to keep all office talks professional, regardless of whether they occur over the water cooler or online.

How to safeguard yourself: Simply avoid involvement. That is the end of the narrative. Nothing positive can come of it. Do not even consider it!

The networker

I'm sure you're familiar with the Networker, who spends more time networking than working. They believe that success is determined by who you know, not what you know. I've spent the entire day watching people network. Almost every day, one guy worked from 8:00 a.m. until 10:00 p.m. At first, I assumed he was a diligent worker. One afternoon at happy hour, many of his employees showed up, and I inquired why he worked so much. He spent the entire day strolling around the company, talking with everyone, and then working after hours.

How to safeguard yourself: Avoid being drawn into a Networker's web. They refer to one another and appear to be connected. In reality, they are merely time swindlers. They squander a significant amount of your valuable time engaging in pointless office chitchat. Everyone quickly grows tired of them. Associating with them will add little to your value.

The taskmaster

Have you ever met someone at work who spends their entire day worrying about what everyone else is doing while simultaneously moaning that no one else in the organization ever does anything, and they are forced to cover? This is the Taskmaster's position. Taskmasters are fast to delegate jobs to avoid having to perform them themselves; and yet, after work is accomplished, the Taskmaster is present to claim credit.

The Taskmaster is continually giving the impression that they are so busy they cannot possibly fit anything else into their day. In actuality, they have a mile-wide lazy streak and strive to avoid work more than most of us to complete our given tasks. How to safeguard yourself: Be cautious of them. Maintain a safe distance from them, or you will spend your days performing their duties.

39

The wakeboarder

Take heed, someone is approaching! Wakeboarders, like Taskmasters, enjoy delegating labor; yet, unlike Taskmasters, Wakeboarders conceal their BS beneath an outgoing demeanor. Because coworkers like them, they are more inclined to assist, the Wakeboarder is aware of this. They spend a lot of time socializing, not to build a network but to discover naive coworkers to whom they can delegate tasks and avoid being exposed.

When a Wakeboarder faces an impending deadline, you'll see them organizing their troops and assembling every conceivable resource to assist them in completing the task or project. How to safeguard yourself: As with the Taskmaster, avoid wakeboarders. While wakeboarders are often excellent employees who generate high-quality completed products, they leave a mile-wide wake as teammates bust their humps to assist them with their projects.

Consider the productivity cost of these workplace BSers and their ilk, not to mention the overall morale of their employers. What matters is that you do not become entangled in their foolishness. Develop strategies to defend yourself and receive the credit you deserve, avoid spending late hours to complete your tasks, and being a victim of their schemes. Work smarter, and you'll always come out ahead.

Interview Questions to Avoid a Job in a Toxic Workplace

The interview questions to ask to determine if a workplace is toxic: It's easy to overlook a potentially hazardous opportunity, all that much more so if you're not seeking it.

Employers have traditionally controlled interviews through interrogative strategies. They retain power due to the scarcity of jobs and their ability to regulate the process. Today, it is a candidate-driven market, with only 6.3 million job seekers and 7 million job openings.

However, many job seekers are unsure of the appropriate interview questions and thus find themselves in less than optimal and occasionally toxic situations. Job seekers need to keep in mind that an interview is both a way for employers to get to know them and get to know each other. The most common mistake made by job applicants is failing to use the interview to ask questions or asking the wrong questions. As a result, they wind up in a culturally-incompatible position. This leaves people feeling trapped, as it is too late to pull out because they have no other plans.

You may have regret for leaving a job, where things weren't necessarily horrible, but you were no longer challenged or had reached the ceiling for advancement. You interviewed with a new employer, and everything appeared to be fine; but upon joining, you discovered the complete opposite. As a result, you have resentment toward your new job, and you despise yourself for being ignorant. Every one of us has been there. You are not alone in this.

To obliterate harmful work environment societies and reestablish certainty, this segment leads you through vital inquiries to assist you with uncovering possibly poisonous work environments.

Positive reviews should be taken with a grain of salt
To begin, conduct research before the interview to gain a feeling for the company's culture and personality. Internet review sites like Glassdoor, Indeed, and Kununu can be

used to accomplish this. Negative reviews should not be dismissed as the work of a disgruntled employee. I've observed businesses bribing, pressuring, and encouraging staff to write nice Glassdoor ratings. Additionally, I've witnessed businesses engage third parties to generate favorable reviews to drown out the negative ones. Is it moral? No, however, businesses are aware of the impact unfavorable reviews have on a candidate's decision-making.

If you notice a pattern of similar statements in poor reviews, inquire about it. For instance, "I saw a few internet evaluations referencing a top-down gossip culture and a terrible work environment. Could you elaborate on it and the steps you're doing to correct it?

Several red signs to check for in their responsibilities include the following:
- Do they disparage the unfavorable reviewers?
- Do they fully avoid answering the question?
- Do they converse in circles, make excuses, and never respond?

This demonstrates that they have done nothing to address the issue and refuse to recognize it as a problem. A company constantly attempting to improve will admit when they have made a mistake, explain what occurred, and walk you through how they intend to rectify it. Most crucial, pay close attention to body language. 93% of communication is non-verbal, with only 7% being spoken. If they're rolling their eyes, appear annoyed, or appear uneasy, make a mental note of it.

Ascertain that they preach what they preach

Recognize your values and research the company's. Businesses should include them on their website. While most businesses profess to live their beliefs, many do not. It is your obligation to determine whether they have them during the meeting, so you don't wind up working for a business whose convictions are at odds with your own.

For instance, I once interviewed with a company that boasted about its open and honest business methods. They inquired about my wage requirements during the phone screening. I provided them with my range, just as I did in my application. Additionally, it should be mentioned that I always conduct research and check that my needs are market-compatible, which they were.

The interviewer answered that my range fell short of their requirements and I needed to submit another application. I requested they divulge their salary range to determine the extent of the discrepancy between my criteria and their budget. They declined, and the interviewer pressed me to alter my pay range once more. If a corporation preaches transparency, how come they cannot provide a pay range when their competitors do?

At this point, I realized I would be unable to proceed with the interview. You may think this is childish, but I want you to consider what else they may claim to do yet fail to deliver. What more are they concealing and keeping secret? How can you trust someone evasive during an interview regarding their wage range?

I refused to proceed with the interview; and oddly enough, they've contacted me twice to get me to reconsider. Despite their efforts and the opportunity's attractiveness on my resume, I was rejected. Maintain your commitment to your principles and avoid allowing the thrill of the position to cloud your judgment.

Determine the role's necessity
The process by which the role became available is one of the most telling indicators of a poisonous culture. You can ascertain this by inquiring whether it is a new or replacement role. If a replacement position, inquire about what happened to the former occupant and why they left. If they turn to trash-talk the preceding individual, this demonstrates a toxic culture. Employers are put off by candidates who speak negatively about their previous employer, so why shouldn't candidates be put off by interviewers who do the same thing? If they are fast to point the finger at a former employee, how quick will they be to point at you or someone else?

Discover what kind of leader are they
There are several ways to accomplish this. If the recruiting manager and another employee or the team are in the same room as the interview, monitor the team or employee in the manager's presence. Is the manager perceived as authoritative, while the team appears hesitant and fearful to speak up? Is the management failing to include them in the discussion or are they inviting them to respond and offer questions? This is a red flag. Your relationship with the management will continue to be the same.

Here are a few additional questions to elicit information about the type of leader they are:
- How do you communicate feedback?
- What kind of leadership style would you describe as yours?
- How do you reinvest in your employees' development?
- Do you have a professional path that leads to this position?

44

- Now that you've gotten to know me, what would be the most difficult obstacle I'd likely encounter in this role/company?

Additional questions to consider:
- How would you describe the culture? (Ensure this is not a generic response and that they explain it. If they refuse, press them further by asking, "Can you explain what you mean by..." or "Can you elaborate on that?"
- How does onboarding work?
- What are the next steps?
- How quickly do you require this position to be filled?

I encourage you to look into their responses in further detail. An interview should be a two-way interaction between the interviewer and the candidate. You should rest assured in your assessment of whether or not they you a good fit. Accept no offer if you have reservations. Utilize this time to conduct an interview and learn about the situation you're about to enter. I've worked in a hostile work environment with a manager who pressured me to ignore all the red signals during the interview, which were numerous. That is not what I wish for you.

What You Can Do To Combat Workplace Negativity

Negativity has a detrimental effect on numerous aspects of the workplace everything from employee engagement to productivity, and even staff retention. Nobody enjoys working in a hazardous work environment, end of the story. Combating negativity is not an insurmountable obstacle, but you need to approach it strategically. When individuals congregate around the water cooler, things get a little more complicated since they can hide behind their laptops and not think about the ramifications of their comments or behavior.

As an individual, you can effect change and eradicate negativity. Combating negativity begins with a single action. Will you be that person? The only thing needed is a desire to start and a willingness to stand up for what is right.

Educate rather than criticize
Too frequently, our response to witnessing or experiencing poor or undesirable conduct is either to ignore it or complain. While these are natural reactions, they also are very ineffective. To have an impact and effect change, you must act and educate others. When you notice negative actions, call them out, but consider that criticism is not the same as action. You must educate individuals about the process through which they can turn negative behaviors into positive ones.

Numerous unpleasant behaviors are unintended and go unnoticed by the person exhibiting them. Interrupters frequently are unaware of how disruptive they are. Individuals who make insensitive remarks may believe they are amusing. Inform them of the unfavorable consequences of their behavior. Demonstrate to them the immediate repercussions of their actions and assist them in changing. Similarly, be aware of your behavior and serve as a constructive role model.

Refuse to participate
If you overhear someone speaking harshly, refrain from engaging in the discussion. Either interject and try to reframe the topic or change the subject. These are your choices. It's all too tempting to join the group and participate solely for the sake of conformity. What is the

harm? The disadvantage is that the more people engage in negative commentary, the more widespread it becomes. Add something nice to the conversation and attempt to lead it in a more fruitful direction.

Speak your mind

Take a stand against negativity and speak out. You cannot affect change if you remain mute. Have discussions about any undesirable actions observes. Consider why we tolerate those harmful actions in the first place. It is simply because negative conduct is permitted or people look the other way, but it does not mean it must continue. Confront the uncomfortable conversations, and stand firm in an attempt to achieve change.

Don't go it alone

If you observe unpleasant behavior, the likelihood is that you are not the only one. Locate others who are prepared to speak out. A single voice causes a ripple, a group of voices generates waves, and a large number of voices generates a tsunami. There is strength in numbers, so make an effort to connect with as many people as possible. Utilize the numerical strength of your organization to accelerate transformation. The more individuals you can train to watch for harmful behaviors, the more quickly you will notice changes in the workplace. By following these steps, you can become a catalyst for positive change at your company.

Suggestions for Coping with a Toxic Workplace

According to a 2019 study conducted by the American Psychological Association, workplace toxicity is not only on the rise, but it also has a significant negative impact on employee mental health. How? According to another study conducted by academics at Lund University in Sweden, toxic work conditions have contributed to increased depression, substance addiction, and other health problems over the last two decades. Simply put, toxic workplaces are unappealing and unhealthy. However, short of quitting your job and looking for another (which may be the best course of action under certain circumstances), there are ways to alleviate the stress associated with working in a toxic office.

Seven strategies for coping with a hazardous work environment are included below.

1. Avoid sinking to the level of a toxic colleague
Assists in combating toxic badmouthing
In other words, avoid rewarding undesirable behavior. When your teammate begins berating your shared boss for his propensity to leave 45 minutes early, resist the temptation to chime in (we know, it's tempting). Rather than that, it offers a neutral response and shifts the conversation to a new subject. Once they understand you're not going to participate in the badmouthing sessions, they're likely to hunt for another venue (aka with a receptive audience). Hopefully, your dismissal will also convey that the behavior is out of the ordinary. Alternatively, lovely. Or admired.

2. Resign from your job at the front door
Assists you in establishing limits in your work-life balance
It's one thing to periodically express your frustration with your partner or roommate about how much work is killing you, but it's quite another to make it the focal point of every conversation. Consider how frequently you discuss your career with loved ones and ensure that most of your chats are not about your cunning desk mate or micromanaging boss. Even if your friends and family truly care about your

48

well-being, they'll become tired of hearing about your work woes. In addition, focusing on the things you can't control is detrimental to your health. People, it's all about finding a healthy equilibrium.

3. Recruit positive coworkers
Assists in fostering a more positive work atmosphere
The odds are that even among the toxic coworkers you've encountered, yet others understand your point of view. Suppose you observe a colleague experiencing similar difficulties and attempt to evaluate their feelings about the situation without gossiping (which will just backfire). Once you've established common ground, you'll be able to lean on one another and commiserate.

4. Confrontation practice aids in very intense, one-on-one confrontations
If tensions have risen to a critical level, it may be time to confront the problem directly. It's frequently difficult to express what you want to say in stressful situations, so practice first with a close friend familiar with the scenario. Your monologue can be improved by running through your points in advance (your employer is continuously expecting too much of you, your supervisor is constantly claiming credit for your ideas, etc.)

5. Establish trust
Aids in dealing with micromanagers
The problem with having a micromanager boss is that it pits our drive for autonomy against their desire for control, two essential human brain wants. Confidence building is the key to overcoming this dispute. You can't gain independence until they get certainty. To earn a micromanager's trust, you must supply them with the three things they seek most: information, inclusion, and control.

Refusing to do so—or being careless with the details—will exacerbate the situation.

Consider the following options: To begin, try to predict what they might want. The better you understand their expectations, the more proactive you can be in addressing them, thus eliminating their need to micromanage. Second, communicate clearly and frequently. This entails sending regular updates and status and progress reports in advance of your boss's request. Bear in mind that this might be as basic as a daily email, listing all your projects and their status or as easy as CCing them on pertinent emails. Finally, make every effort to adhere to their norms. You want to tailor your work to their preferences, discover what quality indicators your supervisor desires/needs, and then meet them. (This may entail conducting an assessment of yourself and identifying any red flags that keep your supervisor from trusting you.)

6. Change jobs or departments
Assists in resolving unresolvable poisonous situations
Due to unstable employment markets and financial obligations, quitting one's work in favor of a healthy environment is not always an option. The decision to look for a new firm may be advantageous if you can do it. Even if now is not the best time to make a move, it never hurts to master the art of networking. Here are some methods for growing (or sustaining) your professional network, whether you're feeling constrained by the pandemic or are an introvert who fears networking. Note that this does not always require you to leave your firm entirely; sometimes, simply changing departments or teams will do wonders in distancing you from a poisonous workplace. If there is another department you are interested in, send out feelers to see if a position is available. You can even spin the

rationale for your team switch to make it appear as though it was your narcissistic boss's brilliant idea.

7. Find outside activities to relieve stress

This benefits your overall mental health

Make sure your life outside work is enjoyable if quitting your career isn't an option at the moment because you have more control over it. This may include scheduling a vent session with a friend who works in a similarly toxic job, taking up a relaxing pastime such as yoga, or prioritizing self-care (a post-work bath, anyone?). The objective is to ensure that, regardless of how irritating your 9-to-5 is, you have something to look forward to once you clock off each day.

CHAPTER 2: A SURVIVAL GUIDE FOR TOXIC WORKPLACE ENVIRONMENTS

Many of us consider our workplaces to be second homes. We spend most of our waking hours at work, and our coworkers are often our closest confidantes. Numerous investigations and research have established that it is physically impossible to be effective and fulfilled in a poisonous workplace environment. Even if you work from home, the spillover of negativity from a toxic workplace may penetrate physical barriers. The intangible qualities that define a good or unhealthy workplace can affect every area of our lives, from our relationships and physical health to our self-esteem, and how we view ourselves as a whole person.

Indeed, the entire scenario, which includes heightened stress levels associated with working in a dysfunctional office or setting, can directly result in job burnout, particularly for emotionally invested people who use it to demonstrate their sense of self-worth.

Why certain groups are more affected by toxic workplaces

- Those with heightened sensory sensitivity are significantly more concerned over "odd events."
- Those who are more sensitive to others' criticism or harsh behavior might quickly be weakened by toxic people's criticism or harsh behavior.
- Those who are excessively conscientious or place a great deal of pressure on themselves to perform have a

sense of obligation to ensure that everyone around them likes them and is content with their work.

- Those who are hyper-aware of everything going on around them may develop an unhealthy state of perpetual vigilance, which becomes emotionally taxing.

- Those who have previously been told they are "too sensitive" or take things "too personally" may now be fearful of speaking up and asserting themselves.

- Those prone to become overworked and anxious are further taxing their already overburdened neurological system.

8 warning signs that your workplace is toxic

Wouldn't it be convenient if there was a simple way to determine if you are caught in a poisonous work environment? Here are eight potential "alarm bells" that may alert you to the fact that you are working in a hazardous work environment.

1 - To put it another way, you should consider yourself "lucky" to be employed

The answer to this one should come as no surprise, don't you think? Line managers who make statements like this should be a major red flag. This potential threat is a scare tactic designed to coerce you into remaining in a marginalized position. It often indicates an organization that depends on bullying and command and control systems to eliminate decent and personalized creativity and free thought.

2 - Inadequate communication

This is another simple one to level at most organizations; however, in the case of the poisonous workplace environment, it is deliberate, internalized, and deliberately encouraged. So, do you feel you're being kept in the dark about critical information? A persistent lack of communication characterizes the majority of toxic workplaces. It's possible that you won't get any response at all; or if you do, it will be harsh and critical rather than encouraging and supportive.

While you may be performing the duties of two, three, or four persons, it is not uncommon for your supervisor or coworkers to claim credit for your accomplishments.

3 - Everyone has a negative attitude or pattern of behavior

If you arrive at work and everyone else is gloomy, pessimistic, and servile, you are locked in a toxic atmosphere. There is no enthusiasm in this environment; no one comes in smiling, and no one ever says, "I love working here." Additionally, it is common to find a high turnover rate among employees, which is a solid clue that people are leaving quickly, most likely due to their dissatisfaction and low morale at work. Consider how many people begin and depart within six to nine months; these individuals have it figured out.

4 - There is always some sort of drama going on

Though cliques rule your work environment, it may feel like you're back in elementary school. You may be worried and paranoid that your coworkers speak negatively about you. Toxic, cliquey coworkers are most often observed loitering around the vending machine, whispering in one another's ears. They have the potential to make what should be a nice employment environment appear nasty and dog-eat-dog. Rumors and gossip are constant at the office; miscommunication, favoritism, and infighting are the norm.

55

5 - Dysfunction reigns!

In your professional environment, do meetings feel like a waste of time that inevitably devolve into disorganized mayhem in which nothing is accomplished. Actions are either not pursued, owned, or taken away? Are the operations, work systems, and business procedures disconnected and failing? Unreasonable expectations and deadlines, a lack of focus, and a sense that "this is how things have always been done and it will never change" are hallmarks of toxic work environments. If new policies or regulations are frequently added, or if the leadership and management teams are never available to assist in resolving issues, these are signs of a broader problem caused by ineffective leadership and low morale.

6 - You have an authoritarian leader

Isn't this far too simple? You can spot them a mile away! This is typically the type of employer who is constantly attempting to exert control over your every move and makes you feel as if they are waiting to pounce on you for making a mistake. Toxic bosses frequently appear unwilling to listen to others and are adamant that their way is always correct. Could it be that your employer takes pleasure in leveraging their authority and demonstrating to others that they are in charge? Perhaps they are unwilling to lend a hand, assist with tasks, or give you credit for a well-done job. If you believe that your boss would want you to come to work even if you were on your deathbed, you might be facing a despotic and poisonous boss.

7 - There is no room for expansion

This is a classic warning sign of a workplace that contains a hazardous stream. If no one appears to have the opportunity for development, growth, or new experiences, you are trapped in a toxic environment. Suppose you've approached your leaders or supervisors, or even human resources multiple times about a lack of recognition and growth possibilities (such as promotions, secondments, work shadowing, coaching or mentoring, and tough assignments) but have received no response. If that's the case, it's time to call it a day.

8 - You simply "sense" that something is a little "odd"
When your intuition warns you that something is wrong, believe it! Physical symptoms such as insomnia or a racing heartbeat may indicate that your sensitive nervous system is alerting you to danger! So take notice!

How to remain sane in a toxic workplace
Because quitting quickly is not always a possibility, here are some suggestions to help you improve your circumstances while you work on your exit strategy.

DON'T:
- Allow negativity to triumph. Simply reflecting on how awful your job is can keep you in a gloomy frame of mind and discourage you from recognizing solutions.
- Take part in the drama. Convince sympathetic allies to join your cause. Spend as little time as possible with harmful or toxic people or gossipers.
- Reduce your boundaries. Take a complete lunch break. Avoid responding to emails after business hours or working on weekends.
- Fail to be your advocate. Consider relocating harmful components of your job imaginatively, such as by delegating, changing managers, or transferring teams entirely.

- Do not be afraid to capture instances and events that bolster your knowledge of toxicity. Maintain a record of any inappropriate or abusive behavior so you may report it if necessary.
- You will lose your sense of "self." Pursue another outlet for mastery, momentum, and fulfillment, such as a hobby.

DO:

- Utilize your property as a proving ground. You'll get the opportunity to practice and develop critical skills such as assertiveness, conflict resolution, and uncomfortable talks.
- Seek assistance. Develop a confidant circle within your job or through a professional group or peer network. Consider collaborating with a seasoned coach. You require trustworthy allies who can act as a sanity check.
- Establish a positive work environment. Surround yourself with images, words, and colors that inspire relaxation or joy.
- Plan your exit. Concentrate your efforts on the next steps and locate something better.
- Take control of your inner self-talk; it may be compelling! Remind yourself that this is a transient situation and reframe your perception. This is not a crisis; it is a test. Your boss is not awful; they are simply immature emotionally.
- Bear in mind that your job does not define you. Examine your ideas and your commitments outside of your job position.

How to Survive a Toxic Workplace: 8 Suggestions for Control

While all organizations have their share of difficulties, a poisonous work atmosphere might feel like an endless Monday morning. It's mentally and emotionally exhausting and prevents you from enjoying your work. Frequently, unwarranted arguments arise, as well as a lack of respect and sensitivity along with punishment for exercising your rights. Even prestigious work environments can be toxic, such as the infamous Ellen DeGeneres program. Quitting is not always an option, which is understandable. The easiest method to ensure that you remain sane during your job tenure is to learn how to withstand a poisonous environment.

What is a toxic workplace? — a checklist of toxic workplace behaviors

If you're unsure whether your workplace is hazardous, it helps to grasp the hallmarks of a toxic work environment. If you're concerned about your workplace's health, you can use this checklist to get an idea.

1. Experiencing burnout

Toxic work settings can overburden you with tasks and thoughts, leaving little time for rest. Even though you put in long hours expecting to be appreciated, your efforts may go unnoticed. Occasionally, you may feel burnout if your job is undemanding and offers no opportunity for advancement or if you're exhausted after working nonstop for an extended period.

2. Inadequate work-life balance

To be effective, you should find some kind of harmony between your own and more proficient lives. Overworked employees in toxic jobs feel guilty about taking a break since they are so overburdened. While eating dinner, you may find yourself working longer hours and checking your email. Relationships outside of work may begin to erode. Passive-aggressive conduct from your supervisor is common during vacation time.

3. Communication that isn't effective

Effective communication is critical to a company's success. As an alternative, communication is scarce and nonexistent in toxic settings. You may find that vital information is being withheld from you by supervisors and coworkers who pretend to have forgotten. Occasionally, your supervisor will provide little to no feedback; and when they do, they will find methods to insult you or criticize your performance without providing any constructive comments.

Other traits include:
- Leaders who do not listen well
- A lack of clarity in the circumstances
- A large number of employees hear contradictory instructions

Conflicts might arise due to inadequate communication, requiring you to remain silent when you ask inquiries.

4. Cliques

A poisonous job might make you feel like you're back in high school. Certain employees may intimidate, exclude, and gossip about others. They share inside jokes, dinners, and breaks together yet alienate everyone else. When they require something from you, they are remarkably nice until the job is completed, and they move on. Unfortunately, coping with cliques is unavoidable for surviving a poisonous work environment.

5. Poor leadership

Having a toxic boss is a strong indicator of a toxic work environment. A toxic boss may yell at you, insult you, or engage in passive-aggressive behavior without cause. Additionally, they may demand you to work long hours without compensation, delegate their personal life to you, and communicate outside of business hours. Certain managers may send emails at midnight and expect immediate responses, while others may phone and expect a fast reaction.

Other bosses are micromanagers content to point out errors in your job and prevent you from concentrating on it. Additionally, you may have a manager who blames you for their errors anytime a senior points out and pretends not to know you exist, frequently forgetting or misspelling your name.

6. Toxic colleagues

Negative people at work are nothing more than a distraction and a nightmare to work with. Different sizes and shapes are available. Some are constantly on the lookout for you, probing for your thoughts and passing them along to your managers or spreading tales about you in the workplace. Others take over your space.

Certain coworkers are constantly playing office politics in the hope of snatching all advancements, while others would not hesitate to take a job offer from you. Other coworkers are a nightmare due to their lack of motivation and laziness. They frequently delegate most of the job to you but claim credit when the boss arrives. Understanding how to deal with these types of coworkers will assist you in surviving a hazardous work environment.

7. Stifled growth

While not all firms offer enormous growth potential, hazardous employment frequently offers little opportunity for advancement. Occasionally, your superiors and coworkers may deny you promotions for which you are very qualified. Other supervisors will not allow you to work autonomously, frequently insisting on excessive supervision, and some will refuse to enroll employees in job-related development programs. Any attempts at self-development, such as taking on additional duties, requesting raises, or enrolling in evening studies are treated with hostility.

8. High turnover of employees

If a substantial percentage of your coworkers decide to leave their jobs, the climate in the workplace is likely toxic. Employees may be willing to work in an office for an extended period to acquire crucial skills, climb the corporate ladder, or advance. However, if people depart after only a few months on the job, there is something wrong with the workplace.

9. Discrimination

Racism is destructive because of discrimination based on race or ethnicity or gender or religion or sexual orientation, age, handicap, or general appearance. Unfortunately, you may encounter prejudiced people against you, alienating, blaming, micromanaging, disrespecting, and denying you opportunities.

Surviving in a dangerous workplace

When attempting to endure a toxic environment, it is critical to remember that certain factors are beyond your control. It's best to take care of what you can and realize that some issues are beyond your control. With that in mind, let us examine your ability to deal with the poisonous work culture.

1. Never bring work home with you

If you've developed a habit of bringing work home, it's time to say no to work files on the dinner table. Bringing negativity into your home when you want to relax and spend time with your family or friends is unnecessary. When the day is done, learn to say no to additional jobs and leave any files or pending emails at the office.

Leave all bad energy at the office, and develop the ability to say "no" when your supervisor proposes you "stay a little longer tonight." Never check your email after hours and avoid calls from managers who refuse to respect your personal space.

2. Identify sustaining coping mechanisms

Discover healthy strategies to divert your attention away from work and cope with stress and worry. If you're comfortable, invite a friend, partner, or spouse to listen to you gripe about work. Communicating with another person can assist you in releasing pent-up frustration and avoiding emotional outbursts at work. If you're unable to speak with someone, consider maintaining a journal or recording private voice notes in which you complain about your job.

Apart from talking therapy, try running, visiting a park, swimming, or walking a dog. Go food shopping, cook, have a snack at a local café, or sit by the beach if time permits. Make sure you leave the office promptly and engage in a peaceful and delightful activity to assist you in coping.

3. Stay away from the drama

If you work with negative coworkers and authoritarian supervisors, make every effort to avoid drama. Maintain a safe distance from cliques and gossip. Only discuss work-related issues with toxic employees and avoid drinks after work with toxic coworkers. This is not to say that you should not defend yourself, particularly when someone is being unpleasant. Yes, speak up and express yourself assertively but quietly. Ascertain if the disrespectful individual recognizes they have crossed a limit and can address issues without being rude.

4. Define boundaries

Toxic workplaces can sap you in various ways, which is why you need strong boundaries. When it's time for a break, savor every minute in stillness. Take vacations as needed and refuse to take work home. If a colleague utilizes your belongings without permission, confront them directly and politely request to leave your belongings alone. Establishing strong boundaries will go a long way toward assisting you in surviving a hostile work environment.

5. Practice mindfulness: Remind yourself of who you are what you have set as goals whenever you have the opportunity, whether at home or work. Surviving a hazardous job is much simpler when a clear objective and deadline have been established. Continue to remind yourself why you're in the position, and if you have an escape plan, use it to get through the day. Most crucial, remind yourself that you are not your job and exist apart from it.

6. Infuse your workspace with positive energy

Your mind needs regular reassuring messages that everything is fine. Surround yourself with cheerful, bright, and beautiful memories. Utilize images from your graduation, relatives, friends, or bright notes that make you smile. Additionally, you can retain these memories if a supervisor disregards your boundaries and becomes disrespectful. Maintain a pleasant attitude by escaping to your happy place in your thoughts.

7. Put any misunderstandings to rest

If a coworker or supervisor is antagonistic toward you, set the record straight and ask why. Leave no space for supposition, even more so when your reputation is under attack. Approach the accountable party to ensure that you either end the conduct or find a way to brush it aside. Surviving a hostile workplace is difficult but not impossible if quitting is not an option. Maintain a positive attitude, set boundaries, and consider why you work there in any case. More importantly, establish routines and behaviors that will assist you in coping with job-related stress and anxiety. Eventually, you'll want to quit the poisonous work environment and seek employment elsewhere as a last resort.

Strategies for Surviving in a Hazardous Work Environment

Despite increased awareness and education, harmful workplaces persist. Additionally, while each work culture is unique, some features of toxic work environments are universal. Take a closer look.

Symptoms of a toxic work environment
Profit over people

Businesses in which personnel is viewed solely as a tool to an end. Employees are frequently assigned additional labor for the same salary. When a team member is let go without being replaced, the remaining members of the team are forced to assume additional responsibilities.

Fear-based

Businesses where fear is the primary motivator. Employees report feeling uncomfortable on the job. Fear and intimidation are employed to effect change and profit. Employees are discouraged from raising concerns and advocating for change.

Rights are irrelevant

Organizations that do not take employee rights seriously. Discrimination, inequitable treatment, and many forms of harassment occur.

How to Survive in a toxic workplace

Numerous intelligent, capable individuals may find themselves working in a toxic culture. In many situations, the organization was not poisonous when they began working there. Mergers, acquisitions, and mismanaged rapid expansion can result in a negative shift in culture. If this is the case, you are not to blame. If you find yourself working in a toxic workplace, it is critical to have a positive outlook while you consider your next steps. Anxiety and tension keep us from seeing the brighter side of things, making it impossible to picture a better future.

The following are some recommendations for navigating a hostile work environment:

1. Revert to fundamentals

It is more critical than ever to attend to your body's basic demands: drink water, eat healthy food, and move your body daily. Establish some structure by keeping water and nutritious snacks nearby and scheduling time on your calendar to go for a walk or workout.

2. Develop a strong morning routine

Becoming more optimistic in the morning will help survive any difficulties that may come your way. Journal, meditate, do breathing exercises, or listen to a pleasant video or podcast to start the day off correctly.

3. Barriers
Consider creating a barrier between yourself and any harmful persons or situations you meet at work. This will protect your energy.

4. Take a moment before reacting
If someone or an email irritates you, avoid the impulse to respond immediately; instead, take five minutes or wait until the next day. Even a brief pause will assist you in responding in a manner respectful to both yourself and the other person.

5. Use a mantra
I like to remind myself that "this, too, will pass". Repeat this mantra silently or aloud whenever you are in a difficult circumstance or feel stressed or concerned.

6. Seek assistance
During challenging times, rely on your friends and family for assistance. If you're having difficulty gaining clarity, working with a professional coach who can assist you in going forward can be beneficial.

7. Locate a constructive outlet for your negative feelings
Crying, pounding a pillow, and exercising are all effective methods of releasing anger. You can also scribble anything you want to say to the person/situation that enraged you and then burn what you wrote.

8. Consider the bright side
Consider the benefits of your current location. It could be financial security, engaging with a coworker you enjoy,

assisting clients, or simply having the scenario serve as a learning opportunity to help you improve.

9. Finally, remember that "this is only a job"

The job is not who you are, but while our jobs/careers are critical, they do not have to affect our self-esteem. If you are unable to quit your toxic work environment, the tips above will assist you in maintaining a healthy mental state. Maintaining a positive attitude amid hardship conserves mental energy, allowing you to focus on determining your next steps and putting your best foot forward in interviews with prospective companies.

CHAPTER 3: A GUIDE TO NAVIGATING OFFICE POLITICS NO MATTER WHERE YOU WORK

Politics is often a taboo topic in the workplace to prevent causing division among coworkers. However, it doesn't mean that they don't happen at work.

What is workplace politics?

In its simplest form, office politics is about interpersonal conflicts at work. These disparities can be in terms of viewpoint, personality, authority, or power. While workplace politics can be challenging to navigate, they are necessary for any firm. However, when bad workplace politics fester, your organization may suffer. Here's how to navigate corporate politics and transform unfavorable workplace culture into a positive one.

Office politics is a term that refers to the complicated social structure that exists within a workplace. It entails employees abusing their authority and power and delegating to advance their agendas. Everyone has a unique job within the microcosm of any company. Regardless of whether you know about it, organization governmental issues direct who has power and impact inside the association.

At the best of times, office politics keeps a team together. The structure is necessary for all organizations, and office politics may offer it healthily and sustainably. It can propel the business forward through social capital. In the worst-case scenarios, those in leadership positions exercise their authority over others. This might result in workplace scorn and resistance. The trick is to ensure that the structures serve the common good. Not just those at the apex of the hierarchical structure.

Six suggestions for improving your office politics
Regardless of their position in the office, nobody can ignore business politics. They are an inescapable reality of existence. You may be intimidated by the thought. However, learning how to maneuver through office politics might assist you in retaining some personal influence. All the way, you'll get a greater grasp of the system in which you work.

Social dynamics mostly drive business politics:
- How you engage with people
- Who you interact with
- When to pick your battles

Whether you favor office politics, they are an unavoidable aspect of the job. Even while they can take on a life of their own, they are not required to be negative. When the timing is right, the flow of knowledge, power, and influence in the workplace can be used to your advantage and that of others.

Let's look at some strategies for improving your workplace political skills.

1. Acquaint yourself with official and informal networks
There are two primary network subdivisions in business politics: formal and informal. The term "formal network" refers to a position of authority or job title, such as CEO, manager, or intern.

The informal network comprises employees who hold little but significant positions of authority behind the scenes. Comprehending both will assist you in determining how to manage each network.

2. Establish beneficial work relationships

It's significantly easier to deal with business politics when you have strong, positive relationships with folks in your immediate vicinity. Loyalty and friendship are two virtues that can lead you far. In the game of social politics, the objective is to develop a support network that benefits both you and the individuals in it. This way, you may be assured that you will have social ties to pull should you find yourself in a rut.

3. Maintain a professional tone

It's critical to be friendly with your coworkers to foster a community at work. However, there is a narrow line between being friendly and sharing excessively. By disclosing excessive information about oneself, you risk people using it against you. Try to maintain a friendly yet professional manner at work unless there is a compelling reason to do otherwise. By establishing limits with your coworkers, you may establish defined work frameworks. Additionally, it protects you from being used by your colleagues.

4. Strengthen your soft skills

Soft skills, on the other hand, are fundamentally refined social abilities. Active listening, teamwork, and good communication are all necessary job abilities. Enhancing your emotional intelligence and other interpersonal abilities enables you to maneuver more deftly through office politics.

5. Advocate for yourself

It can be challenging to be courageous and have your voice heard. However, knowing when and how to advocate for oneself is an invaluable talent to possess. Speaking up when you or someone you know is being treated unfairly demonstrates your fortitude. Additionally, it will make office bullies less likely to target you.

6. Keep an optimistic attitude

While everyone has difficult days, no one enjoys a workplace downer. Working long hours may be a hard and exhausting experience, both psychologically and physically. However, ranting in a non-constructive manner about your concerns will be distracting for others. Keeping a cheerful attitude at work may boost your likeability. Additionally, it will facilitate collaboration with coworkers.

Five strategies for resolving toxic workplace politics

When persons in positions of power use their influence over others for personal advantage, bad office politics begins. Backstabbing, gaslighting at work, and toxic cliques are all far too common in office life. Regrettably, many powerful persons abuse their positions to intimidate and manipulate others. This contaminates the workplace dynamic. Understanding and dealing with workplace politics is essential to a successful career. This will assist you in establishing a more secure position inside the organization. Additionally, it will enable you to assist others in times of need.

Consider the following five strategies for reversing negative politics in your office.

1. Establish a positive corporate culture

The foundation of a functional, pleasant workplace is the company culture. Creating a positive business culture encourages employee motivation and engagement. In addition, it enhances self-esteem and self-worth in one's professional function. Organizations can foster a positive culture by anticipating and meeting employee needs and offering fair opportunities for advancement. A nice work atmosphere fosters positive office politics and protects vulnerable individuals from acquiring ill intents.

2. Promote open, positive dialogue

Promoting constructive, transparent communication is a critical component of sound business politics. To ensure that everyone feels treated fairly and with respect, communication channels must be open. Effective communication decreases the possibility of misinformation spreading. This decreases the likelihood of conflict arising. Communication also contributes to the development of trust among colleagues, improving the development of positive social networks and favorable employee interactions.

3. Maintain a laser-like focus on team objectives

Collaboration and teamwork account for a sizable portion of healthy corporate politics.

Maintain a strong emphasis on team-building activities and getting everyone excited about your company's aims. In this manner, you may eliminate harmful dynamics while boosting company morale. Concentrating on the here and now has a place. However, urging staff to look beyond today will rekindle team spirit. As a result, the likelihood of unwarranted conflict can be reduced.

4. Evaluate the organizational structure of your business

Though businesses are not always aware of it, an unhealthy hierarchy may exist. This hierarchy has the potential to make those at the bottom feel oppressed and unheard. Your business may have a top-down or bottom-up organizational structure. Regardless, it is critical to do regular assessments of your business's structure. Management practices are bound to alter as new managers and bosses come and go. Conducting a corporate structure review may need a change in how things are run.

5. Reward the appropriate individuals

Favoritism is a risky game to play on the job. When employees believe they are being forgotten, jealousy grows in every corner. Favoritism develops a culture of contempt in any workforce.

Rewarding productivity is an excellent method. However, people with reward authority who delegate recognition must ensure that personal objectives or emotions do not cloud their judgment. While preserving a sense of fairness, leaders should distribute praise evenly across staff and establish defined criteria for awarding prizes.

Seven distinct categories of office politicians

Apart from official titles and responsibilities, office politics include a variety of subtle yet distinct functions. Not all roles, such as gossiper, bully, or adviser, are clear. Nevertheless, most of them may be found in virtually any office or business. Each office politician type brings something fresh to the table. However, what they provide is not necessarily beneficial.

This is a list of various office politician types who abuse their power, deliberately generate friction, or utilize their position to obtain their desired outcome.

1. Gossip

Office gossipers enjoy gossiping about others, frequently in a negative or underhanded manner.

Individuals who gossip do not always mean to damage others. However, disseminating other people's personal information may hurt feelings or damage one's reputation. If your workplace has office gossip, try to avoid discussing others' personal lives, particularly if the individual with whom you're conversing is not present.

2. Bully

The presence of an office bully frequently characterizes corporate politics. Bullies exist in every aspect of life, and workplace settings are no exception. Indeed, workplace bullying is increasing. Acquiring the ability to cope with them is a valuable life skill to be applied in and out of the office. A workplace bully acts maliciously toward others. They may threaten team members, obstruct their work, or utilize social influence to sow discord. There are many different types of bullies. From somewhat annoying to seriously endanger the health and safety of their coworkers, their actions have a wide range of consequences.

3. Climber

Climbers, also known as social climbers, leverage their relationships with others to advance their status and social power in business or life. The social climber is never content with his or her existing position. They seek power by using their ties with others. Social climbers can be observed tactically associating with authority personalities in company politics, such as managers and stakeholders.

Social climbers disregard or avoid individuals perceived to be "below" them.

4. Consultant

An adviser's function is to interpret statistics or other pertinent information. They then use this data to assist authority figures in making critical decisions. Frequently manifesting as a manager or assistant, advisers are a critical component of the office politics environment. Advisers wield considerable power since they can exert influence over others in positions of greater authority.

A terrible adviser will utilize his or her influence for personal benefit or exploitation. At the same time, an ethical adviser always seeks to support judgments that promote the greater good.

5. Credit thief

Credit thieves are individuals who take credit or appreciation for another's effort and pass it off as their own. They are not believers in credit being given where credit is due. Rather than that, they prey upon weak colleagues who don't speak out for themselves if someone else claims credit for their efforts.

6. Saboteur

A saboteur is someone who employs sabotage to maintain dominance inside an organization.

They may attempt to derail another initiative to make their own appear better. Or they employ duplicitous measures to guarantee they are not competing with anyone. At times, it can be difficult to uncover a saboteur's schemes. However, employees should always feel comfortable reporting such behavior.

7. Lobbyist

A lobbyist makes concerted efforts to persuade individuals in positions of authority. Lobbyists are perpetually self-interested. They utilize their influence to persuade people to support their cause. Without a lobbyist, no system of corporate politics is complete. They must be recognized before causing damage.

How to Make the Most of Office Politics

Obtaining What You Desire Without "Dirty Playing"

When you hear "office politics," what pictures spring to mind? "Backstabbing," spreading false information, and "sucking up" to the right people? Keep yourself as far away from this as possible if this is the case! However, whether you despise or embrace office politics, they remain a reality of life in any firm. Additionally, it is possible to promote yourself and your cause without jeopardizing your personal or organizational beliefs.

By engaging in "proper" politics, you can advance your and your team's interests fairly and appropriately. Additionally, being aware of "bad" politics around you enables you to avoid unnecessary suffering at the hands of others. This section discusses why workplace politics exist and seven strategies for "winning" without succumbing to the lowest standards of behavior.

Utilize office politics to your benefit while remaining true to your ideals.

What Is the Political Climate in Your Workplace?

To some level, all workplaces are political simply because people bring their emotions, wants, ambitions, and insecurities to work. It's not generally simple to settle on what achievement means or how to accomplish it. When these interpersonal and ideological disputes become too much to handle, office politics arises. And because we are frequently invested in the decisions we make or that others make about us, we want to influence others' choices. We can be straightforward or deceptive in this regard.

Additionally, keep in mind that certain individuals will always have more power than others, whether through hierarchy or other means. While it is natural to want to use or grow our power, we may do so at the expense of others. Finally, organizations operate on a shoestring budget. This might result in teams striving to meet their individual needs and objectives, even if it is counter to the "greater good."

Seven Office Politics Survival Tips

Accepting politics as a reality lays the groundwork to make it positively work for you. It may evolve as members of your organization come and go, but chances are it will never completely vanish. A solid and supportive network can only be built when you've developed strategies to recognize political conduct and understand it.

1. Conduct an organizational chart analysis

Office politics frequently operate outside the confines of the formal organizational structure. Therefore, take a step back, observe for a while, and then map your organization's political strength and influence rather than people's rank or job description. Ask yourself questions like, "Who are the actual influencers?" to identify them. Is there a person who has power but rarely uses it? "Who do people look up to?" Is there anyone you know who is a role model or mentor to others? and "Who are the company's brains?"

2. Acquaint yourself with the informal network

78

Once you've established where power and influence are concentrated, it's time to investigate people's interactions and relationships to better understand informal or social networks. People who are easy to get along with and those who have a hard time making friends should be on your radar. Investigate in-groups, out-groups, and cliques. Keep an eye out for ties founded on friendship, respect, romance, or something else. Finally, attempt to decipher the parties' influence flows and if there are any interpersonal problems or instances of bullying.

3. Establish Relationships

After you've understood how existing relationships work, you may begin developing your social network. Consider individuals beyond your immediate team and across the formal hierarchy — coworkers, supervisors, and executives. Become unafraid of politically powerful individuals. Rather than that, get to know them and form genuine friendships that avoid hollow flattery. Maintain a cordial relationship with everyone, but avoid being overly identified with one group. Additionally, if you consider a personal relationship at work, ensure it is based on consent, there is no implication of illegal or inappropriate influence, and confidentiality is never violated.

4. Strengthen your "interpersonal skills."

As we've seen, strong interpersonal skills are essential if you want to build and maintain a successful political network. Take a look at your feelings, then ask what triggers them and how you handle them. Self-control allows you to ponder before you act. This level of emotional intelligence lets you be aware of and comprehend other people's feelings and their preferred or disliked methods of communicating. Additionally, you must develop a keen ear for listening. You'll find that listening helps you slow down, concentrate, and pick up new information. Additionally, people appreciate those who listen to them!

Tip: Take our quiz to determine your emotional intelligence level.

5. Maximize your network

Through your interactions, you may develop your brand and elevate the visibility of your team.

When you convey your accomplishments to your connections, they may open doors for you, your team, and your boss to "shine." Additionally, they can serve as a "bridge" between you and your colleagues.

Caution: When using your network in this manner, exercise caution since you do not want to develop a reputation as a "pest!" Always keep your organization's objectives in mind and refrain from "badmouthing" others; otherwise, you'll make more enemies than friends. Rather than that, establish a reputation for "positive political action."

Additionally, it is critical to take responsibility for your actions. This exemplifies sincerity and integrity. Therefore, solicit comments from others who may have a unique viewpoint. Finding out what matters most to your network's members is easy with this method, which shows how much you appreciate their opinions.

6. Be courageous but not irresponsible

Your initial reaction may avoid those who engage in "bad" politics. Indeed, the inverse may be more effective. "Keep your companions close and your foes closer" is often involved saying in workplace issues. Therefore, familiarize yourself with gossip and manipulators. Be friendly but cautious, as they may misrepresent what you say. Attempt to comprehend their motivations to minimize or mitigate the consequences of any harmful political maneuvering. Additionally, be aware that some people behave poorly out of insecurity — a type of self-sabotage. However, safeguard yourself against somebody you suspect of Machiavellianism or another of the Dark Triad's qualities. These individuals are almost certainly intelligent and dangerous.

7. Defend against negative politics
You can contribute to a more positive work environment by refraining from "fueling the fire" and engaging in bad politics. For instance, avoid spreading rumors without thoroughly examining their source, trustworthiness, and impact. Furthermore, do not rely on confidentiality. Consider that anything you say will be retold, so carefully choose your "secrets"! Don't get involved in fights or recriminations, and always maintain a professional demeanor. When a disagreement occurs, keep in mind that there does not have to be a winner and a loser. Often, a solution that satisfies everyone is possible.

Be confident and firm when expressing your own concerns or criticism but not confrontational. Additionally, ensure that you adopt an organizational mindset rather than just a selfish one.

Effective Strategies for Dealing with Office Politics

When people work together daily, many lifelong ties are formed, but arguments eventually occur. This is true even when the majority if not all, employees work remotely. Developing the ability to deal with conflict and collaborate is a critical talent that any professional must have.

Here are how employees and leaders can effectively manage office politics, whether they work in the office or remotely.

1. Maintain a sense of reality while remaining compassionate

It's difficult to read your audience when using Zoom or video conferencing. After a meeting, follow up, ask additional questions and extend the benefit of the doubt. Everyone is facing unique obstacles, so flex your kindness muscle. Take the high road if you've witnessed some weird office politics. You want to be known as an ethical leader.

2. Always be genuine

Your greatest value will always be your genuineness. Take your words seriously, keep your commitments, and avoid being a person who always considers public opinion before acting. Authenticity is critical in the workplace. It will elevate you to "trusted" among your coworkers.

3. Develop the ability to listen actively

To successfully navigate workplace politics, you must learn to listen actively. With video chat and email serving as the primary modes of communication for remote employees, it can be practically impossible to interpret another's tone, let alone their motives. The majority of situations develop as a result of incorrect assumptions. Simply "replying" to what you heard with the purpose of understanding should assist you in avoiding potential problems.

4. Pose difficult questions

Individuals will always converse, and some will attempt to elicit your input. When a colleague begins discussing workplace politics with you, inquire, "Have you expressed your concerns directly to that individual?" Do you believe you might accomplish your objective more quickly if you went directly to the source?" It is preferable to have a neutral demeanor on the job and to be renowned for your brilliance!

5. Assume a favorable attitude
Individuals remain the same, regardless if they are at the office or in a virtual environment. In dealing with office politics, I suggest taking the high road. Assume a pleasant attitude and engage in dialogues to ascertain the facts so you can maintain strong professional connections. Assuming a positive intent and attempting to understand will result in swift remedies and a win-win outcome.

6. Develop a service-oriented perspective
Political landscapes will continue to hold sway until others come to perceive things differently. A self-centered vision must give way to selflessness. It must be motivated by love and the desire to serve and see the best in everyone. If one individual does this, others will be perplexed as to why they feel differently. If enough people begin to do so, a tipping point is reached, and the political landscape collapses.

7. Establish a buddy system for new employees
This technique will be successful in establishing a buddy system. It is about linking new hires with the most skilled and dedicated members of the staff to assist them in navigating a challenging environment. This includes a discussion of real and perceived office politics. It is critical to address what is true and offer techniques for dealing with what is truly perceived.

8. Make an effort to maintain cordial relations with everyone
Nothing can sabotage employee engagement more than workplace politics. You can only win if you don't

participate. Make an effort to maintain cordial relations with everyone. Maintain a good attitude and avoid being "Negative Nelly" and "Complainer Carl." Yes, communicate with coworkers but keep your focus on cooperation and solutions. Even if you're forced to work the hallways to advance an idea, maintain your integrity and excellent status with your team.

9. Remain objective in the face of adversity

Today, successfully handling office politics is necessary for any successful professional. It appears to rear its ugly head in our daily lives, even in isolated locations. One effective method for overcoming office politics is to always maintain a neutral position in confrontational situations. By not adding gasoline to the proverbial fire, you can avoid additional confrontation or de-escalate situations.

10. Place a premium on inclusivity and collaboration

Often, it is as straightforward as inclusion and collaboration. A willingness to share ideas, bounce them off others, and get feedback tends to result in less adversarial politics. Involving important members of key departments in your work carries a lot of weight and makes navigating organizational politics worthwhile.

11. Communicate without preconceived notions

When motives and intentions are questioned, office politics flourish. A sincere desire to help others can be demonstrated by making an effort to communicate with others in the organization, whether through chat, email, phone, or a virtual meeting. Something as easy as a chat message or email with the subject line "Hello!" I hope you're doing well!" serves as a reminder to coworkers that your goals are good and encouraging.

Rules of the Game for Office Politics

For some, the term "office politics" is unacceptable; yet in the workplace, it is prevalent. In its simplest form, workplace politics is about disputes between employees; disagreements of opinion and conflicts of interest frequently emerge. All this boils down to human communication and interpersonal interactions. There is no great explanation for accepting an unfortunate work environment. The best performers have mastered the art of office politics.

The following are seven beneficial behaviors that will help you succeed at work:

1. Be aware that you have a choice

The two most prevalent responses to workplace politics are fight or flight. It's a natural human reflex for survival in the wild, dating back to our hunter-gatherer ancestors. While the office is a modern jungle, winning at office politics requires more than spontaneous instincts. Instinctive fight reactions will increase resistance to whatever you're attempting to do, while instinctive flight reactions simply label you as a pushover who can be taken for granted. Neither of these approaches is conducive to good career advancement.

Winning requires that you pick your reactions to situations consciously. Recognize that you can choose your feelings and reactions regardless of the circumstances. Therefore, how do you choose? This brings us to the following point.

2. Knowing what you're aiming toward is essential

When disagreements occur, it's too easy to go into tunnel vision and focus exclusively on immediate differences.

This is a self-defeating strategy. By concentrating on differences in people's viewpoints or ideas, you're likely to attract additional pushback. The method to mitigate this without appearing to be battling for the right to win in this battle is to keep an emphasis on business objectives. Discuss the advantages and disadvantages of each choice in light of what is best for the business.

Ultimately, everyone wants the business to succeed; if the business fails, no one in the organization succeeds. It's much easier to swallow their pride and back down when they understand the chosen course of action is the best for the firm. By developing the ability to influence the discussion in this direction, you will develop the ability to detach from trivial disagreements and position yourself as someone interested in getting things done. Additionally, your manager will develop an appreciation for you as someone mature, strategic, and capable of taking on greater duties.

3. Concentrate your efforts on your circle of influence
At work, there are frequently issues over which we have little control. It is not uncommon to come across corporate policies, client expectations, or supervisor directives that conflict with your objectives. Gossiping and whining are normal responses to uncontrollable occurrences. However, other than providing a temporary emotional outlet, what tangible results do gossiping produce? In the majority of cases, none.

Rather than feeling victimized and enraged by the circumstance, concentrate on what you can do to affect it – on your circle of influence. This is an extremely empowering strategy for overcoming powerlessness. It alleviates victimization and enables others to view you as someone who understands how to function within established limitations. It's possible to feel that you tried your best in a scenario where you had no control over the outcome. Constraints are ubiquitous in the job; by taking this approach, your manager will develop an appreciation for you as an understanding and optimistic employee.

4. Refrain from taking sides

It is easy to find yourself trapped between two conflicting power figures in office politics. You are tossed around as they attempt to outwit one another and defend their positions, all to the detriment of you completing the task. You cannot persuade them to agree on a project's common conclusion, and neither of them wants to take ownership of concerns; they are too terrified of being stabbed in the back for any mishaps.

In situations like this, keep your focus on the company objectives and avoid taking a side — even if you prefer one over another. Put them on a single communication platform and ensure that all parties communicate openly so that no one can claim, "I didn't say it." By remaining neutral, you will assist in objectively directing dispute resolution. Additionally, you'll establish trust with both sides to keep engagements productive and on track with corporate objectives.

5. Avoid getting personal

You will become enraged with persons in office politics. It occurs. Occasionally, you'll have the want to speak your mind and teach someone a lesson. Don't. People frequently recall instances in which they were embarrassed or degraded. Even if you win this debate and feel great for the time being, you will pay the price later when you require assistance. What goes around, especially in the office, comes around.

To succeed at the office, you'll want to develop a network of allies. The last thing you want to happen during a crisis or an opportunity is for someone to screw you over just because you enjoyed a brief period of emotional outburst at their cost. Another motivation to control your outburst is career advancement. Organizations are increasingly embracing 360-degree reviews to promote employees. Even if you are a superstar performer, your boss will face political opposition if other managers or colleagues perceive you as tough to deal with. You would rather not make it harder for your boss to advocate for you.

6. Seek first to understand, then to be understanding
People feel unreasonable when they believe they have been misunderstood. Instinctively, we are more concerned with making others understand us. Top human resource managers and corporate executives have mastered suppressing this impulse. Surprisingly, attempting to understand is a highly effective method for disarming others. Once the other party perceives that you understand his/her perspective, they will become less defensive and more receptive to your perspective in return. This establishes the groundwork for open dialogue to reach an acceptable agreement for both sides. Without this understanding, arriving at a solution is extremely difficult – there is little trust and much second-guessing.

7. Think win-win
As stated, political disputes arise as a result of clashing interests. Perhaps as a result of our education, we are taught that someone else must lose to succeed. On the other hand, we are afraid of losing if we allow someone else to win.

That does not have to be the case in business and at work. Develop an attitude of "how can we both win in this situation?" This demands an understanding of the other party's perspective and what's at stake for him.

Following that, determine what's in it for you. Strive to reach an agreement that is agreeable and helpful to both parties. This will guarantee that everyone makes a genuine commitment to the negotiated resolution and does not just pay lip service to it. Individuals despise defeat. You may get away with using win-lose methods once or twice, but you will quickly lose allies on the job. Thinking win-win is a tenacious strategy that cultivates allies and aids in long-term victory.

Ten Strategies for Avoiding Office Politics

How to Maintain a Low Profile and Avoid Office Gutter Politics Proceed Cautiously

Office politics are a fact of life in the majority of organizations. Competition is unavoidable when employees spend hours together and compete for the same promotions and raises each day. While some argue that office politics are an integral element of the workplace, others argue that they are an unnecessary and potentially harmful component of corporate culture, eroding morale and straining relationships.

Do you know what you can do to protect your personal and professional reputations from being damaged by office politics and gossip?

1. Recall your high school years

In some ways, companies are similar to high school. Generally, the same concepts apply. People form cliques and these play a role in success, but your reputation may be easily ruined if you make a mistake. When you find yourself in hot water over gossip and office politics, consider yourself an adult offering advice to a high school student. What would you tell your adolescent self?

2. What they are unaware of cannot hurt you

It's wonderful to work alongside genuine close friends. However, suppose you, like most individuals, are not that fortunate. It may be better if your coworkers know just enough about you to engage in friendly conversation, but not so much that any knowledge could jeopardize your career. While networking outside of work can help you progress professionally, use caution – one too many drinks and your coworkers will have dirt on you. If you'd like to friend your coworkers on social media, consider adding a "work friends" privacy setting on your Facebook page.

3. Interact with your boss

Are you hoping to be promoted or earn a raise? Allow no one to inform your boss via the grapevine. The majority of managers are overworked, and they seek problem solutions. You can assist your manager by communicating your enthusiasm for advancement. Additionally, your employer may provide suggestions for improvement or the measures necessary to advance your career.

4. Avoid gossip

Gossip is the simplest way to end up in hot water or appear immature. Nothing conveys the message "I am not prepared for a promotion" more than trash talk. While socializing is okay, be aware that whatever you say will come back to haunt you, even more so when someone else gains from it.

5. Maintain current knowledge

There is a narrow line between gossip and keeping up with current events. While you should avoid trashy office chatter, listening to what others say is still beneficial. It will keep you from being shunned. While gossips information is not always accurate, you may pick up on hints about forthcoming promotions or significant changes, such as corporate restructuring, retail closures, or outsourcing.

6. Pick your friends with care

Without some form of social interaction, work becomes unpleasant. If you choose to socialize at work, be selective. If someone constantly speaks negatively about others, consider making friends with a different employee. Who you associate may also affect the decisions made by your boss. If you're known to associate with inefficient staff, this may adversely affect you.

7. Recognize backstabbers

It's critical to recognize gossipers and backstabbers as soon as you begin socializing at a new job. These coworkers may initially wish to take you under their wing, but such "friendship" comes with a cost. Save yourself for a better buddy, who will not speak adversely about you during promotions, reviews, or layoffs.

8. Consider the long-term

Someone at work has been spreading rumors about you, and it's terrible to learn about it. Taking revenge might be exhilarating at the moment, but it's important to look at the bigger picture. Adhere to the high road. You'll benefit in the long run.

9. Avoid venting at work

While having a support network at work can be beneficial, excessive complaining will leave a negative impression, especially if the complaint is about work. If you believe you are being treated unfairly or discover a work-related issue, speak with your manager. The most effective method to receive appreciation for your work is to request it.

10. They are observing you

We are not attempting to instill fear, but when you are at work, you should know that you are being observed and everything is a test. Certain individuals engage in games to determine who is trustworthy. Whether management confides in you with juicy gossip or limits talk to the current project, make no mistake: this is a test. Your performance may have an impact on your career prospects.

CHAPTER 4: THE NEGATIVE EFFECTS OF A TOXIC WORKPLACE ON YOUR BODY & MIND

A "dysfunctional and dramatic" workplace is regarded as a "toxic work environment." Does this ring a bell? If it does, you may find yourself trapped in a terrible workplace. Numerous indicators indicate whether a workplace is harmful. Chronic stress, overwork, and office gossip are all indicators that your workplace may be hazardous. Additionally, if your workplace is toxic, it might hurt your health.

The following are the five most serious health consequences of a toxic work environment:
1. Depressive disorder
According to Mental Health America, depression is one of the top three workplace issues. The majority of the time, employees are blissfully unaware of their predicament. Even if they are aware of the symptoms, a toxic work environment may discourage an employee from getting therapy. Employees may suffer depression, boredom, impatience, headaches, difficulties concentrating, guilt feelings, and other negative emotions that have a detrimental effect on their health. Employees are frequently afraid to seek treatment because their company has instilled dread.

2. Anxiety
The constant fear of work results in anxiety, which can be difficult to manage. Anxiety can impair an employee's

ability to perform their job through bodily symptoms such as excessive worrying, jumpiness, jittery sensations, shaking, and a racing heartbeat. Anxiety in a toxic work environment can result in absenteeism, negative thoughts, overreactions, and an inability to accomplish duties. These are aggravated by the paranoia that frequently accompanies anxiety.

3. Stress
Stress is associated with more than emotional trauma. As Workplace Mental Health notes, stress can result in structural damage to the brain, PTSD, impaired immunological function, and an increased risk of depression. Stress impairs performance, putting the affected employee in a position where they cannot seek assistance.

4. Fatigue
Are you constantly exhausted? This is a regular occurrence on a toxic job—the psychological toll of operating under such duress results in sleep deprivation and even sleeplessness. Excessive weariness can result in a loss of sexual drive, social withdrawal, gastrointestinal problems, and migraines, among other symptoms. Constant fatigue might result in burnout and job loss.

5. Sickness
Many people report feeling sick more frequently when working in a hostile work setting. When combined with stress and weariness, the immune system weakens, making you prone to sickness. Your muscles ache, you may feel as though you have a cold, or you may get ulcers due to the increased stomach acid. When employees' bodies are exhausted, they will miss work, adding to their distress.

According to Professor and Author Jeffrey Pfeffer, "many occupational exposures are just as detrimental to people as secondhand smoke regarding their consequences on self-reported physical health" and mental health. Stress impairs immunity, resulting in illness. Interpersonal interactions that are not healthy might result in emotions of guilt and worthlessness. Toxic work settings have been shown to increase the risk of depression.

The consequences are not limited to the physical. Working in toxic workplace results in a lack of job security, bad work/life balance, and a loss of autonomy. They also contribute to unhealthy habits such as binge eating, excessive drinking, and smoking.

CHAPTER 5: THE DANGERS OF WORKING IN AN UNHEALTHY WORKPLACE

At some point in our lives, far too many have worked in an unhealthy workplace. You may be wondering if you are currently working in an unhealthy work environment. Certain workplaces are hazardous, while others are less obvious. Any profession carries the risk of injury or stress, but the risks are magnified in an unhealthy setting.

In the United States, about one out of every five employees say they have been exposed to hazardous working conditions. I was one of them for far too long. I spent three years at a corporation that did not allow people to grow or utilize their skills, did not provide growth opportunities, and did not even provide water. Early on in my tenure with the organization, I knew that it was a gloomy, demoralizing dead end. At the time, I didn't know that the effects could potentially hurt my physical and emotional well-being.

What a toxic workplace looks like?
If you are enduring mental stress, emotional misery, or physical discomfort, your toxic work environment may be blamed. The first step toward escaping a toxic workplace is admitting that it is toxic and becoming aware of the impacts on your physical and emotional health.

Determine whether you are working in an unsafe workplace by answering the following questions:
- Are you dreading your commute to work?
- Every time you leave for work, do your shoulders ache?

97

- Do your supervisors or coworkers instill in you a sense of self-doubt?
- Is verbal abuse directed at you by supervisors or coworkers?
- Are you fearful of taking time off?
- Is your wage insufficient?
- Is your employment insufficiently challenging?
- Are you overburdened with work while your coworkers slack off?
- Is it unclear what your performance expectations are?
- Is it possible for others to claim credit for your work?
- Is it discouraged to be a team player?
- Is there a shortage of advancement opportunities?
- Does the business not promote and support employee relations?
- Are you not provided sufficient time or assistance to fulfill your tasks?
- Are you discouraged from acquiring new talents that would enhance your resume?
- Is your office a hotbed of workplace gossip?
- Are you discouraged from providing feedback or expressing your opinion?
- Do your employees engage in mutual sabotage and undermining?
- Are your coworkers pessimistic?
- Do your coworkers place blame for their shortcomings on others?

Have you answered affirmatively any of these questions? Even one or two affirmative responses raise a significant red flag. You're almost certainly working in an unhealthy environment. Continue reading to discover more about the indications. If you recognize any of the above, your workplace is poisonous.

Physical dangers of an unhealthy workplace

Certain high-pressure, fast-paced workplaces take a physical toll on employees. This is detrimental since it reduces worker productivity and profits. Employees may be working themselves to death. Several of the physical consequences of an unhealthy workplace include:

1. Carpal tunnel syndrome

According to the Mayo Clinic, repetitive wrist flexion can cause carpal tunnel syndrome by damaging the median nerve or exacerbating any existing damage. A cruel work environment exacerbates carpal tunnel syndrome, a disorder that affects people who spend their days on computers, grocery checkers, and assembly line employees.

2. Back injuries

Inadequate training, incorrect lifting technique, hurrying, and a distorted sense of the dangers associated with lifting are the primary causes of back injuries in the workplace. Once you've sustained a back injury, you're substantially more likely to sustain another in the future. Employers must ensure that staff who lift are properly equipped and trained. A bad job environment ignores such risks.

3. Illnesses as a result of toxic exposure

Workplace exposure to hazardous compounds can negatively affect the respiratory, renal, cardiovascular, and reproductive systems. OSHA requires employers to have processes to minimize workers' exposure to chemical risks and hazardous chemicals. OSHA should be notified of any violations of these rules. Again, a bad work environment ignores compliance.

4. High blood pressure

Working long hours might increase your chance of getting hypertension or high blood pressure. This illness can have several negative consequences for your health, including aneurysms, strokes, heart damage, renal failure, and even vision loss. If you are pushed work overtime, you may need to reduce your hours to safeguard your health.

5. Fatigue

According to OSHA, weariness can hurt one's health. Apart from decreasing your alertness and decision-making abilities, it can also damage your memory and concentration capacity. Additionally, it can make you irritated and unproductive. Fatigue on the job can be fatal if you are a driver or work with machinery, resulting in cardiac problems.

6. Digestive issues

Workplace weariness can sometimes result in digestive difficulties that mimic the symptoms of irritable bowel syndrome. Diarrhea, nausea, constipation, and bloating are all possible symptoms. These symptoms might also be a result of workplace stress. Additionally, work stress can increase stomach acid production, resulting in indigestion and heartburn.

7. Diabetes

Depression, stress, and worry at work can all contribute to the development of type 2 diabetes, which has no treatment. When you are stressed, your body is unable to release insulin. This will eventually result in an abnormally high glucose level in the blood. The longer you are stressed, the higher your blood sugar levels will rise.

8. Injuries occurring as a result of accidents or explosions

Each year, millions of Americans suffer non-fatal workplace injuries, and roughly 5,000 people are murdered. Numerous disabilities are caused by slips, trips, fall accidents, fires, explosions, and violence. Additionally, they cost businesses millions of dollars. Most of them are avoidable injuries that could have been avoided with improved training and equipment. Any of these physical consequences of toxic (dangerous) environments can result in lost pay, missed work, and, in the most severe circumstances, permanent disability. Anyone who has one or more of these health issues due to their job is in an unhealthy workplace.

2 Frequently asked questions about the dangers of an unhealthy work environment on mental health

According to the American Psychological Association, mental health is a fundamental human right and a necessity for therapeutic, legal, moral, and financial reasons. Your entitlement to mental health does not end when the clock strikes twelve.

1. Common Mental Health Risks

Several of the mental health consequences of a toxic job include:
- Stress
- Depression
- Anxiety
- Paranoia
- Anger management difficulties
- Fear

Many people develop unhealthy coping habits such as drinking or overeating to cope with pressure. If you already have mental health issues before working for a toxic organization, the environment may exacerbate existing issues. This is especially true when you are subjected to unjust treatment or believe your supervisor has something against you.

2. Insomnia

Numerous stressed workers report sleeplessness. When you work in a toxic atmosphere with extreme stresses, putting your work behind you when you're not on the clock can be difficult. This frequently results in long, sleepless evenings filled with worry and tension. Additionally, insomnia deprives you of the time to recharge. Without adequate sleep, you may get irritated, making it more difficult to manage stress. Additionally, it can increase your likelihood of making errors or being involved in a work mishap.

How to restore a toxic and unhealthy work environment?

In a toxic workplace, problems often begin at the top. Greed, micromanagement, competitiveness, and undermining are all issues that originate at the ownership and management levels, and it is at this level that reform must occur. The following steps can reverse the condition

1. Enhance your organization's culture

If you prioritize profits before people, your company's culture must be addressed. Examples include exhausting employees through excessive hours and unreasonable demands or pitting employees against one another when employees have more creative control and can accomplish realistic goals and overall productivity increases.

2. Strike the appropriate work-life balance

Routine tasks like going to the doctor or going to a parent-teacher conference can become huge sources of stress for employees who cannot take time off when they need it. If your employees are required to jump through hoops and risk being disciplined for having appointments during work hours, your workplace is toxic.

3. Become familiar with your workers' compensation benefits

If you've developed medical difficulties due to unsafe working circumstances, it's critical to understand your rights and the workers' compensation payments that may be available to you. According to one carpal tunnel injury attorney, if you cannot work temporarily or permanently due to a work-related condition, you may be eligible for disability benefits.

When employers create dangerous conditions that result in employee disability, they incur increased workers' compensation insurance premiums. Having the best company culture possible, sufficient training, employee incentives, taking safety precautions, and providing employees with flex time all help a business boost its bottom line.

Employers can save money and enhance productivity by implementing these actions. If you work for a company that does not adhere to these guidelines, you deserve more. Businesses that provide benefits demonstrate their appreciation for employees. This draws in more talent, which results in increased earnings and employee satisfaction. If your abilities are unappreciated, it's time to move on.

Establishing limits to protect your health

To combat the negative impacts of an unhealthy work environment, you'll need to establish and enforce some boundaries. This will be different for each employee, as each has their own priorities and personal lives. Your boundaries should safeguard your relationships and personal life, and employment.

Communication is one area where limits may make a difference. You should be forthright, direct, and professional in all job encounters. Effective communication will increase your efficiency and reduce the likelihood of miscommunication. Even if you're dealing with the office's biggest jerk, strategic communication has the potential to put him in his place.

Most importantly, if you're going to overcome a toxic work environment, you will have to learn to say "no". That means saying no to the overtime wearing you down, no to taking on the tasks of a slothful teammate, and no to the manager who wants to claim credit for your ideas. Your attempts to establish boundaries may not be well received in an unhealthy setting. Let's face it, and toxic managers do not operate their firms in a way that benefits the staff. Before asserting yourself at work, begin by building a workable Plan B.

Even if you aren't ready to send in your two-week notice, you can start putting yourself out there even if you can't instantly leave a terrible workplace. Refine and update your résumé, begin building relationships on LinkedIn, and watch job advertisements.

Healthy habits to assist you in coping

You do not have to work in a toxic atmosphere to reap the benefits of the following healthier habits. On the other hand, these coping methods must be employed immediately if you operate in a toxic atmosphere.

- Maintain a stress journal: Whenever anything at work worries you, jot it down and describe how you responded. Within a few weeks, a pattern should begin to appear.
- Establish an exercise program: Take lengthy walks, visit a yoga studio, or participate in group sports such as soccer or softball. Any type of exercise can assist you in reducing your stress.
- Get adequate sleep: Regular sleep is necessary for stress management, but it can also improve your performance. Reduce your caffeine intake if necessary.
- Use your vacation days wisely since you need time to relax and recharge. You worked hard to get those days. When you return to the office, you may acquire a new viewpoint.
- Develop relaxation skills: You may wish to practice deep breathing exercises, develop a meditation habit, or cultivate awareness to learn how to de-stress from work.
- Speak with your boss: Create a plan for coping with workplace stress and explain to management how you will carry it out and why it will benefit you.

Everybody needs to let it all out now and then, especially when dealing with job stress. Whether it's a weekly lunch with friends or a relationship with a trustworthy therapist, you need to establish a support system on which you can rely. If you're having trouble obtaining the support you need to modify your patterns, consider consulting a psychologist who will provide additional assistance with stress management.

CHAPTER 6: WHY DO HARMFUL WORK ENVIRONMENTS FOLLOW YOU HOME?

Working outside the office should contribute to the de-escalation of workplace toxicology. However, in reality, a dysfunctional working atmosphere may deteriorate even further when you return home. When Nikolina left the workplace in early 2020 to work from home, she believed the toxic culture at her company would improve. "I assumed my job would be significantly less stressful without my employer scrutinizing my every step," said the 22-year-old content writer located in Prague. "I was completely incorrect."

Rather than that, her supervisor devised new methods for monitoring the team electronically through software such as TeamViewer and Hubstaff. Nikolina, who has requested anonymity owing to privacy concerns, believes that the lack of colleagues nearby affected him since the supervisor became obsessive about micromanaging every aspect of his working hours and finding the tiniest flaws to criticize. "Our stress levels were elevated by the knowledge that our supervisor might check on us at any time, and we were collectively going insane."

For people working in hazardous office environments, the transition to remote work may appear to be the silver lining of COVID-19 and an opportunity to enjoy much-needed separation from a poisonous environment. However, as Nikolina experienced, unpleasant work dynamics can follow us home, and in some cases, exacerbate the difficulties associated with working with employers or colleagues who behave badly.

Toxic work cultures can significantly influence employee wellness, which is why employees must understand their protection alternatives.

Toxic from the top down
Toxic workplaces take numerous shapes, but they all share one characteristic in common with their employees: negativity and injury. According to Aditya Jain, an associate professor of human resource management at Nottingham University Business School, the term "toxic work culture" refers to a workplace where employees are exposed to psychological hazards. "They may lack or lack organizational support, have bad interpersonal interactions, an excessive workload, a lack of autonomy, inadequate compensation, and job security."

Our stress levels become elevated our employers check on us. According to Jain, the repercussions of such a work culture are far-reaching. They may include physical health consequences such as heart disease or musculoskeletal illnesses, poor mental health and burnout, and organizational consequences such as decreased attendance, engagement, productivity, and innovation.

Many poisonous work cultures are the product of poor management, whose harmful habits are easily spread. An associate professor at Villanova University's management and operations department in Pennsylvania, US, who has studied abusive bosses and toxic workplaces, says: "Destructive actions from the top trickle down. When CEOs exhibit toxic behavior, the rest of the organization assumes the behavior is acceptable and participates in it.

Soon enough, a toxic climate develops in which everyone believes, 'This is how we do things around here.'"

Before the pandemic, toxic behaviors occurred in the workplace during meetings, presentations, and casual interactions. They now occur during phone calls and text messaging. And while you may expect that being away from the office might alleviate some of these pressures, researchers say the opposite is more likely.

"Toxic cultures endure in remote situations, as seen by identical antagonism expressed via Zoom conversations or email," Priesemuth explains. Anonymity and distance can magnify unwanted behaviors; it is sometimes easier to deliver a disrespectful or threatening message by email or text message than to express it in person." Another contributor to poor behavior is pandemic weariness. "Psychological anguish and depletion are significant contributors to workplace aggression. "Perhaps people simply have shorter fuse lengths, resulting in less respectful contact and discourse," she adds.

In Nikolina's instance, her boss' previously restrictive behavior began to feel more like harassment than monitoring after she went remote. "At random intervals, he would phone and demand that you share your screen or that we screen record our entire day. If he spotted a prolonged period of inactivity, he would initiate a Zoom check-in or TeamViewer session, even while folks attempted to shower or cook supper." She claims he regularly messaged employees at midnight with urgent requests and prevented them from taking days off. "Under his leadership, my entire staff suffered," she explains. "I was constantly anxious and had difficulty sleeping at night, staying up late thinking about work."

Top-down destructive behaviors have a trickle-down effect per Manuela Priesemuth. According to experts, having a bully boss can be especially detrimental in remote work circumstances, as many are currently experiencing. According to Jain, the individual must still interact with the bully but may find the behavior more difficult to manage at home due to a lack of social connection, emotional tiredness, and the work-life imbalance caused by blurring personal and professional lines. "Working remotely might exacerbate the situation since the individual may be unable to seek informal social support from coworkers or utilize HR's grievance channels due to their isolation and a diminished sense of empowerment," he adds.

Coping with a toxic culture
According to Jain and Priesemuth, you are eliminating toxic work cultures requires businesses to identify and treat the core causes of the dysfunction, which frequently turns out to be poor management. Although this does not mean that employees must sit back and wait for things to improve, they should not. An important first step is to educate yourself on your rights, whether outlined in your employer's employment policies or local laws.

"Being aware of your employer's legal obligations is beneficial because it enables you to hold them accountable," Jain explains. Numerous countries regulate working hours, vacation time, and holidays, with the United Nations' International Labour Organization's rules acting as a global standard. "Knowing this might be beneficial in dealing with bosses whose remote-work demands are unrealistic or unjust." Be sure to keep all correspondence, including emails and phone calls that may contain evidence of harassment or other forms of unprofessional conduct if you've been subjected to it.

"Accumulating proof of antagonism can be a valuable tool for substantiating any charges made to human resources or senior management," Priesemuth explains. "It's also useful to seek out allies, possibly coworkers who have had similar experiences or have witnessed violations – who can act as a support system or assist in resolving the issue."

However, banding together with colleagues will only get you so far if there is no genuine human resources department or grievance procedure in place, as in Nikolina's small company. "Concerns and complaints could not be raised because there was no human resources department or leadership to turn to," she explains. "Our supervisor was our sole contact, and his attitude was one of gratitude for our positions and salaries. Finally, I resigned, along with many others, after the pandemic began creating distant positions. Now that I've gained creative freedom and peace of mind, I can launch my own business, a dating and relationship website."

If shifting professions is not an option at the moment, you can take steps to reduce your vulnerability to toxic behaviors. "Stronger boundaries between work and personal life have proven beneficial for employees," Priesemuth explains. "Research indicates that it can help employees cope with job-related stress and improve overall well-being." While this might be extremely difficult with a toxic employer, you can begin by taking tiny steps such as turning off your phone after a particular time in the evening, signing out of email, and making yourself inaccessible.

Priesemuth emphasizes that these coping mechanisms may only lessen the impacts of a hazardous remote work environment momentarily, not permanently. If your company's leadership finally fails to listen to feedback and implement change from the top down, toxicity will almost certainly endure, as will your anxiety and fear. Naturally, each employee's circumstance is unique, and not every person has the same amount of wiggle room for change if any at all. Whatever your circumstances, it's critical to realize how detrimental toxic work settings can be, whether remote or in-person. Just shrugging off unpleasant surroundings will only exacerbate the problem. While solid boundaries, social support, and stress management may all be beneficial, you may want to consider moving on eventually if things do not improve. At the very least, these tactics can buy you time until you get a more advantageous position.

CHAPTER 7: A TOXIC WORKPLACE CAN HAVE A NEGATIVE EFFECT ON YOUR MENTAL HEALTH IN 12 WAYS

Every morning, the annoying shrieking of your alarm clock is your least favorite sound in the ENTIRE WORLD! It sends shivers down your spine, fills you with fear, and any motivation you may have had before the phone rang has completely vanished. By the time you're ready to leave, you've essentially compelled your feet to take you where you need to go. What is causing you such distress? "Now, I'm off to work. No, today is not particularly horrible." Indeed, every day is a poor day in your place of employment. It is extremely poisonous. There are cliques and gossip, and those in positions of authority misuse their power and speak down to you. You feel imprisoned, fully helpless, and completely alone!

A toxic workplace or a toxic employer can negatively affect your mental health. It can transform you into a soulless zombie from a person pursuing your passion. However, we assure you that you are far more adorable than a genuine zombie! In fact, MUCH cuter. Therefore, let's learn how to deal with a toxic work environment and the influence it can have on mental health! Consider the following as your checklist for a toxic workplace:

1. Anxiety
Work should not make you uneasy. Yes, stress is a natural aspect of most occupations, as are deadlines and the need to perform well all of which are quite natural! However,

worry and anxiety should not be generated by your coworkers. A professional shift may be in order if you're concerned about cliques and how your coworkers may treat you.

2. Depressive disorder
The disarray! The suspense! The depressive episode! It's all connected. Working in a toxic work environment or culture can take a toll on your mental health and lead to depression. Constant negativity prevents you from developing positive associations with your work and the people around you. If you work 40+ hours a week in an office with toxic coworkers, you're bound to be depressed! You should leave work feeling energized, optimistic, and content! You should not feel the need to cry constantly.

3. Negative self-contemplation
When anything terrible occurs during our day, we tend to cling to it. It's difficult to let go! Therefore, when you're trapped in a terrible environment every day, it's difficult to avoid replaying the day in your thoughts! This is referred to as negative ruminating. Rumination of the negative reinforces any negative thoughts about yourself, your workplace, and your coworkers. Even if you have a nice job experience, the negative ones seem to take over and make you forget about that sliver of positivity.

4. Your inner critic makes an appearance
A poisonous work environment will frequently make you forget how amazing you are! Negative work environments make it difficult to accomplish the job well! It's especially challenging when your superiors or bosses provide little favorable feedback regarding your performance. Understandably, this is a setting conducive to the

flourishing of your inner critic! It's difficult to let rid of negative self-talk when there isn't any, to begin with!

5. Exhaustion

Burnout is an extreme state of mental and physical tiredness. Even the concept of unlocking your PC seems inconceivable! A hostile workplace can rob you of your life! There is no opportunity for recharge and nothing with which to recharge! It's the equivalent of attempting to fill an empty cup with air. It simply does not work!

6. You have a sense of purposelessness

Humans are wired to want to make a difference in the world through their work! No matter how big or small, the desire to make a difference is universal. However, if you are locked in a workplace that saps you of any happiness you may have gained from your career, it may feel as though you lack the purpose you seek.

The hostility might become so overwhelming that you lose sight of why you initially adopted this position. It begins to feel useless, and you lose motivation and a sense of direction in life. That is not what I wish for you! I want you to constantly feel certain of your direction, wherever: north, south, east, or west!

7. You are easily irritated

Being readily irritated, easily aggravated, or even a little angry are all-natural reactions under stress. Your body and mind are attempting to process many environmental and emotional stimuli simultaneously, which can be exhausting. Therefore, if you're wondering why you have a shorter fuse when working, this could be the reason!

8. Your sleep is impaired

Did you know that anxiety and stress can affect quality sleep? Yep! If you noticed a change in your sleep pattern after beginning employment in a harmful environment, it could be why! You may have become so desperate for a good night's sleep that you've experimented with nearly every sleeping product available. However, a new mattress, melatonin, and all the lavender-scented goods in the world are proving ineffective because your body is reserving stress. Thus, when sleep arrives, the worry, anxiety, and tension you experienced throughout the day (together with the negative rumination) force you to miss out on some much-needed shut-eye.

9. Sunday night scares

Since you began experiencing negative feelings at work, you've lived your life in fear. You're only working to get money for the weekend! You like the time away from work, and you dread returning the next day when Sunday night arrives. If you were wearing boots, they would be trembling. Without warning, the Sunday Scaries will be in FULL FORCE!

10. You undervalue yourself and your work

When coworkers and managers at work consistently underestimate you, you begin to believe that you are not good — or intelligent — enough to accomplish your job. You're trapped in anxiety that causes you to lose faith in yourself and your talents! It's easy to feel that your work is worthless, has no impact, and makes no difference. It makes you feel insignificant and as if no matter how hard you try, you will never measure up.

11. Increased addiction to substances

Anxiety and worry can make you want to drink or take other substances to ease the pain. I get it! At times, you just need to unwind, and the only way to do it is with the assistance of a glass of wine at the end of the day. However, I encourage you to exercise caution if you notice this pattern. You may be developing an addiction to an external substance as a means of relieving stress. Assuming this is the situation, you should use solid survival strategies and stress relievers. Perhaps doing kickboxing once or twice a week or simply screaming into your pillow will suffice! (Have you ever waited until you were the sole vehicle on the highway before screaming? It's incredibly cathartic!) Whatever is effective! But be cautious not to develop an addiction to a substance that assists you in managing stress when it gets unmanageable.

12. Self-defeatism

Occasionally, we willfully sabotage ourselves after YEARS of crap. Occasionally, we deliberately self-sabotage with defeatism to avoid having making the difficult decision to quit and let our employer bear the brunt of our termination. Whether intentional or not, self-sabotage jeopardizes any goodwill developed with other people and departments. Do not let your hard work up to this point come undone because you became the workplace gossip, trashed colleagues, were irresponsible with critical or confidential information, procrastinated, or became ruthlessly disconnected from others.

I hope none of these examples rings true. However, if they do, you may be working in a harmful environment. I trust this assists in deciding the sort of work environment you chose to work and focuses you into taking the correct direction. You deserve to THRIVE, not simply survive.

117

CHAPTER 8: CONGRATULATIONS ON LEAVING A TOXIC JOB. NOW THE HEALING WILL BEGIN

Raydiance Dangerfield, who worked as a learning and development specialist in Maryland at the time, began to doubt her abilities after seeing her friends gain promotions while she was overlooked. On top of that, facing a steady onslaught of microaggressions from her peers altered the way she developed — and felt about — her professional relationships. She eventually left her employment but did so with a sense of paranoia and suspicion.

Working in a toxic workplace characterized by ostracism, incivility, harassment, bullying, and other actions on the part of leaders, supervisors, and coworkers reduces productivity and performance, erodes collegial relationships, and is related to stress and burnout. Toxic settings can also have a detrimental effect on employees' life outside of work, leaving them emotionally fatigued and experiencing decreased well-being and greater conflict at home.

Therefore, quitting a toxic workplace as soon as possible is a wise choice. However, taking that step does not always imply overcoming it. Even if you find a new career or move to a new city, you can't help being reminded of the past. Unless you face trauma full-on, it will become another bag you have to carry around that you never intended to have.

You, like Dangerfield, may find a new career after enduring a bad environment. This one is unique—new people, a new atmosphere, and possibly new job responsibilities—but it

119

does not negate a previous experience. Perhaps you're nervous about meeting a new manager since your previous boss was a bully. Or perhaps you lack the confidence to speak out in meetings due to being hushed at your previous gig, which made you feel unsafe to enter the discussion.

The poison from your prior toxic workplace might linger in your body. However, if you want to start over and advance your profession, there are steps you can take to leave the toxicity behind. Bear in mind your "why." "To maintain perspective, consider why you left your prior position and chose your new one," advises psychotherapist and well-being specialist Farah Harris, LCPC.

Identifying why you left teaches you about boundaries, Harris explains. "Was it due to a micromanager's micromanagement or racial aggressions, or was it due to a lack of efficient communication?" Suppose you've identified the toxic behaviors that drove you from your previous employment. You can determine whether these same patterns are present in your new one or whether your prior experience influences how you perceive and react to the present.

"Once you become aware of and acknowledge your emotions, you can make more informed, conscious choices rather than allowing them to subconsciously shape your viewpoint and behavior," says Dangerfield, now a career counselor and owner of My Curated Career. And when it's not only about why you left but also what you saw in your new company that convinced you to take this job. Your emphasis I has narrowed to what is a true fit. Clarifying your expectations of your boss and coworkers will aid in long-term performance and the ability to maintain a happy view of life.

Dive deeper

"At times, you may leave a toxic work environment unaware of the extent to which it has impacted you until you become triggered in a new location," Harris explains. Identifying your triggers, for example, such as being purposefully interrupted during team meetings or put under the bus by a team member is simply the beginning.

"You must be self-aware; you cannot just state, 'This [manager's or coworker's behavior] causes me anxiety.' Why do you feel anxious?" Harris asserts. Suppose a supervisor micromanaging you causes you anxiety, for example. In that case, you may dive deeper to discover that you value autonomy. When that barrier is violated, a negative reaction occurs—all the more unpleasant since you have previous experience with a manager violating that boundary.

Journaling or freewriting about such feelings might be beneficial, Harris suggests. To begin, use the following prompts:
- What is the most difficult or unsettling emotion you have to deal with at work? Explain.
- Consider a previous period in your professional life when you experienced comparable unpleasant feelings and write about it.
- Re-examine the incident that prompted you and jot down the facts without elaborating.
- Is there a particular emotion that you wish to experience (or experience more of) at work?

Consult management

Open communication with your manager helps alleviate concerns about bringing unpleasant feelings from a past job to a new one, so don't hesitate to bring it up. This does not mean you should go into your former employer's office and vent about your former boss, Harris notes. A verbal dump that lacks defined objectives may destroy your reputation. Rather than that, concentrate on what will help you succeed. You'll be on the same page about expectations if you're able to explain how they can get the most out of you," Harris says.

Remember when you recognized your triggers and the reasons for your reactions? The more self-aware you are, the easier it gets to advocate for yourself. Additionally, employing highly specific language helps you stay on track and express what will work best for you in your new job. Use direct language, such as "I am in my zone of genius when..." or "I tend to accomplish my best job when..." to speak with your manager about how they can help you. "That is the vulnerability aspect, and it might be a little frightening," Harris explains. However, "a good leader will actively listen to determine how they can reassure their staff, pay attention to what is said, and follow up with consistent check-ins to ascertain the person's progress and provide constructive comments."

Establish a support network
If you find yourself glancing over your shoulder at your new employment, Dangerfield suggests reaching out to your network or cultivating a new one. A personal board of directors or a professional network could offer guidance and support. In this way, you will see if your trauma is manifesting in your new employment or if you're genuinely confronting harmful behaviors.

Also, since you've experienced a sad and detaching experience that can negatively affect your life both at and outside of work, supporting proficient and individual connections during your recovery is even more basic.

But remember that even the most well-intentioned mentor or friend may not have the capacity to help you at this critical moment. "Secure the services of a career coach. They can assist you in developing a clear vision for your career and developing a strategy," says Dangerfield, who sought assistance from both a career coach and a therapist in her search for a healthy work environment. As career counselors, they can help you evaluate new opportunities, such as navigating the process of establishing limits in a new role. A mental health expert can accomplish the same thing and can also assist you in developing new behaviors and connections as you recover from old events.

A toxic workplace has lasting repercussions that are difficult to overcome. However, utilizing a variety of tactics will assist you in recovering, allowing you to use this chance and jumpstart your new professional life.

CONCLUSION

According to a 2019 study conducted by the American Psychological Association, workplace toxicity is not only on the rise but has a significant negative impact on employees' mental health. How? According to another study conducted by academics at Lund University in Sweden, toxic work conditions have contributed to increased depression, substance addiction, and other health problems over the last two decades. Simply put, toxic workplaces are unappealing and unhealthy. However, short of quitting your job and looking for another (which may be the best course of action), there are ways to alleviate the stress. Seven strategies for coping with a hazardous work environment are included below.

1. Avoid sinking to the level of a toxic colleague: assists in combating toxic badmouthing
In other words, avoid rewarding undesirable behavior. When your teammate begins berating your shared boss for his propensity to leave 45 minutes early, resist the temptation to chime in (we know, tempting). It offers a neutral response and shifts the conversation to a new subject. Once they understand you're not going to participate in the badmouthing sessions, they're likely to hunt for another venue to do so (aka with a receptive audience). Hopefully, your dismissal will convey that her behavior is inappropriate.

2. Resign from your job at the front door: assists you in establishing limits in your work-life balance. It's one thing to periodically express your frustration with your partner or roommate about how much work is killing you, but it's quite another to make it the focal point of every

125

conversation. Consider how frequently you discuss your career with your loved ones, then ensure that most of your chats are not about your cunning desk mate or micromanaging boss. Even if your friends and family truly care about your well-being, they'll become tired of hearing about your work woes. In addition, focusing on the things you can't control is harmful. It's all about maintaining a healthy balance.

3. Seek out positive co-workers helps with creating a more positive environment: assists in taming negativity. There is a good chance you're not the only one who feels negatively about your coworkers. Suppose you observe a colleague experiencing similar difficulties and attempt to evaluate their feelings about the situation without gossiping (which will just backfire). Once you've established common ground, you'll be able to lean on one another and commiserate.

4. Confrontation practice: aids in very intense, one-on-one confrontations

If tensions have risen to a critical level, it may be time to directly confront the problem head on. It's frequently difficult to express what you want to say in stressful situations, so practice first with a close friend familiar with the scenario. You might improve your monologue by rehearsing it ahead of time if your boss demands too much of you or your supervisor continuously claims credit for ideas that you came up with.

5. Establish trust: aids in dealing with micromanagers
The problem with having a micromanager boss is that it pits our drive for autonomy against their desire for control, two essential human brain wants. This conflict can be resolved

126

by building trust. You won't be able to take control of your life unless the other has clarity. To earn a micromanager's trust, you must supply the three things they seek most: information, inclusion, and control. Refusing to do so—or being careless with the details—will exacerbate the situation.

Below are a few ideas to ponder:

- To begin, try to predict what they might want. To avoid micromanaging, you need to know their expectations and address them before they arise.
- Second, communicate clearly and frequently. This entails sending regular updates and status and progress reports before your boss's request. Bear in mind that this might be as basic as a daily email listing all your projects and their status or as easy as CCing them on pertinent emails.
- Finally, make every effort to adhere to their norms. You want to tailor your work to their preferences, discover what quality indicators your supervisor desires/needs, and then meet them. (This may also entail assessing yourself and identifying any red flags that keep your supervisor from trusting you.)

6. Change jobs or departments: assists in resolving unresolvable poisonous situations

Due to unstable employment markets and financial obligations, quitting work in favor of a healthy job is not always an option. A new firm may be worthwhile for those who think beyond the box. Even if now is not the best time to make a move, it never hurts to master the art of networking. Here are some methods for growing (or sustaining) your professional network, whether you're

127

feeling constrained by the pandemic or are an introvert who fears networking.

This does not always require leaving your company; sometimes, simply changing departments or teams will do wonders for distancing you from a poisonous workplace. If there is another department you are interested in, send out feelers to see if a position is available. You can even spin the rationale for your team switch to make it appear as though it was your narcissistic boss's brilliant idea.

7. Find outside activities to relieve stress: this benefits your overall mental health.

If quitting your job isn't a possibility right now, make sure your life outside of work is fulfilling and something you have control over. This may include scheduling a vent session with a friend who works in a similarly toxic job, taking up a relaxing pastime such as yoga, or prioritizing self-care (post-work bath, anyone?). The objective is to ensure that, regardless of how irritating your 9-to-5 is, you have something to look forward to once you clock off each day.

www.ingramcontent.com/pod-product-compliance
Lightning Source LLC
Chambersburg PA
CBHW030524210326
41597CB00013B/1023